Tao of Wing Chun Do: Volume 1
Part 1
By James DeMile

Tao of Wing Chun Do: Volume 1 Part 1
By James DeMile

Copyright © 2025 I&I SPORTS SUPPLY. All rights reserved. Published by I&I SPORTS SUPPLY

ISBN 978-0-934489-27-0

Acknowledgments

To Bruce Lee, for helping me understand, Jesse Glover, Bruce Lee's first assistant instructor, for sharing his skills and friendship, John Beall, for his many personal contributions to the development of WCD

Dr. L.V. Biffer, Ph.D., an invaluable colleague

Photo Acknowledgments

Kimo Wong, Dominic Gonzalez, Jesse Draughon, Paul Walker,
BiD Sode, Lee Sode, Bob Anderson, Irene DeMile, Sifu James Clark,
Korbett Miller, Shaun Pochik, Kamal Shamoun, Kwok Tom,
Dennis Stom, Rocco Ambrose, James Calvin, Marc Haire, and Paul Chessare

SPEGAL ACKNOWLEDGEMENTS

It was easy for me to write this book;
unfortunately, as origiiiany written,
no one could understand it but me.
To Helen Sutkus and Irene DeMile,
my editors,
who made this volume readable and practical.

DISCLAIMER

Please note that the publisher of this instructional work is NOT RESPONSIBLE in any manner whatsoever for any injury which may occur by reading and/or following the instructions herein. It is essential that before following any of the activities or instructions, physical or otherwise herein described, the reader or readers should first consult h/s or her physician for advice on whether or not the reader or readers should embark on the physical activity described herein. Since the physical activities described herein may not be appropriate, be too sophisticated or strenuous in nature, it is essential that a physician be consulted.

PUBLISHED BY: I&I Sports Supply Co., Inc. from original work by Si jo **James W. DeMile** of Wing Chun **Do**
Design **& Artwork** by I&I Sports Supply Co., Inc.

PREFACE

The roots of the Tao of Wing Chun Do go back over 400 years. Early Wing Chun was developed for two reasons. One was to create a means by which the mind and body could unite harmoniously through a series of simple and efficient exercises. The second was to create a practical means of defense against the bandits who were common in that area at that time.

From this early beginning. Wing Chun evolved to the Shoalin Monastery, Hong Kong and finally to the United States. During this journey, Wing Chun established a series of unique, practical, traditional techniques. To this day, these techniques are practiced widely throughout Mainland China and Hong Kong.

Bruce Lee, who was an early exponent of Wing Chun, brought to the United States a new concept in martial arts training. He eliminated the need to follow traditional guidelines and replaced them with creative learning principles. In a short period of time, he was able to adapt and modify the basic principles he had previously learned in his martial arts training into what may be termed "modern Wing Chun".

The author, who trained with Bruce Lee in the early 1960's, has his Master's degree in Psychology and his doctorate in Hypnotherapy. In the late 1960's, he combined his interpretation of the modem Wing Chun as learned from Bruce Lee with the modern science of behavior modification. The result of this combination was a dynamic program for personal development known as Wing Chun Do.

In the later years of the author's own development, however, he became aware of the limitations of conventional training programs as related to the total development of man. So he expanded Wing Chun Do into a way of life, thus the Tao of Wing Chun Do.

The Tao's program helps anyone who is interested in achieving spiritual fullfilment. The program makes the individual aware of his mind-body potential and contributes to his confidence in expanding his ability to handle all levels of social interaction and communication. This confidence allows him to function with more internal harmony and enhance his total spiritual evolution.

The Tao believes that the essence of one's being is to evolve his potential as related to daily situations. Rather than to act in servitude to an intangible force, one's energy should be directed towards expanding his limitless potential by eliminating the barriers and restrictions that impede personal growth.

The Tao does not inflict either religious or philosophical concepts on the individual. Its only purpose is to offer a variety of techniques by which any individual can become aware of his own thoughts and feelings as related to his personal existence. Unlike other organizations of a spiritual nature, the Tao approaches the spiritual development of the individual in an indirect manner. In this way there is no threat to one's conventional beliefs.

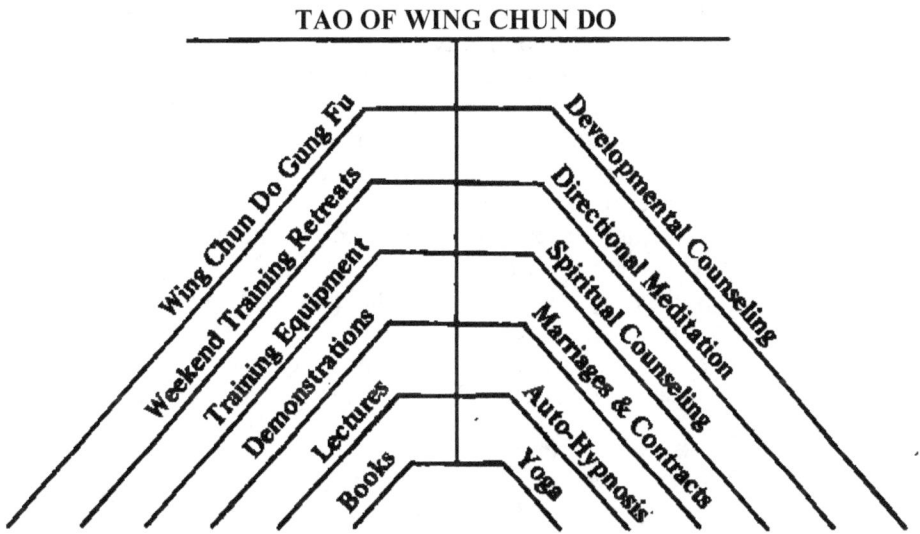

TAO of WING CHUN DO
SYMBOL

The three solid lines on the top signify Yang (black), male: extreme hardness, strength, firmness, dominance.

The three broken lines on the bottom signify Yin (white), female: extreme softness, yielding, subtleness.

The three lines on the ri^it (solid line in the center, broken lines on the outside) signify Older Sister, soft and yielding on the outside but with an inner firmness and strength.

The three lines on the left (broken line in the center, solid lines on the outside) signify Older Brother, finn and strong on the outside yet springy and flexible on the inside.

The center design is a deviation of the Yin and Yang. The white tail extending around the black area and the black tail extending around the white area help to distinguish individuality; but by one encompassing the other harmony and endless continuity are shown. i

;The eyes of opposite color in each area signify that no matter how strong something is there *should* be some gentleness within; no matter how soft something is, there *should* always be some strength within.

Yin and Yang represent the traditional way of life catering to the established and accepted standards and customs.

Older Brother and Sister represent the non-traditional or changing way of life. Not being restricted to tradition and form, they seek to expand themselves by using only techniques and principles that complement total personal growth.

The spaces between each trigram show that each is an individual; the circular pattern shows that each individual belongs to the same family.

TABLE OF CONTENTS
Volume I, Part 1

FOREWORD/8

INTRODUCTION / 9

CHAPTER 1 -ORGANIZATION AND STRUCTURE OF A MARTIAL ARTIST /11
Clarification of "Martial Artist", Game Plan

CHAPTER 2 -BREATHING AND MEDITATION / 21
Breathing — Savansana, Complete, Cleansing and Vitalic Breath
Meditation — Indirect, Direct, Key Word, Control and Direction of Breathing, Power Meditation, Paper Meditation, Meditation for Speed, Imagery Meditation, Candle Meditation, Vase Meditation, Complementary Exercises

CHAPTER 3 -STRETCHING / 41
4-Way Stretch, Sun Salute, 4 Counting Aloud Exercises, Single Arm Extension, Ma Bo-Gung Bo, Cat Stretch, Knee Bend, Single Leg Stand, Back Bend, Jackknife, Knee Presses, Forward Bend, Upper Thigh, Inner Thigh, Standing Side Splits, Wood Block Stretch

CHAPTER 4 -POWER EXERCISES, STATION TRAINING, TRAINING SCHEDULE, TECHNIQUE CALENDAR /57
Power Exercises - Wrist Roll, Tiger Push-ups, Hand Grips, Stretch Spring, Double Doan Chi, Slow Punching with Wrist Roll, Heavy Bag, Skipping Rope, General Suggestions Station Training — First and Second Stations Training Schedule — Time Schedule, Sample Complete Training Schedule, Blank Training Schedules, Sample Training Schedule Technique Calendar — Sample

CHAPTER 5 -NINE CRITICAL PERIMETERS / 79
Upper, Lower, Lower Gate, Inner, Outer, Extended, Right, Left, Kill Range, Blending of Perimeters, Joan Som

CHAPTER 6- STANCES / 88
Balance and Weight Distribution, Open Bi Jong, Closed Bi Jong, Left, Right, Reverse Closed Bi Jong, Single Unit Moving Technique

CHAPTER 7 - BASIC HAND PRINCIPLES / 101
Perimeter Control: Blocking vs. Clearing the Gate, General Comments, Superior and Inferior Positions, Palm Phon Sao, Taun Sao, Fook Sao, Goang Sao, Die Jeong, Pak Sao, Lop Sao, Bong Sao, Hueng Sao, Bil Jee

TABLE OF CONTENTS
Volume I, Part 2

POWER BASE AND SPEEDi Application of Power Base, Power Speed, Actions and Reactions.

HAND STRIKING PRINCIPLES AND THEORIESt Double Chung Choie, Chop Choie, Single and Double Bil Jee, Qua Choie, Short Hook, numb Strike, Jun Jeong, Elbow Techniques, 1 and 3 Inch Floating Punch. Double Pak Sao Technicpe, Foreann Joint Breaking Technique, Striking Targets and Surfaces.

OFFENSIVE LEG TECHNIQUES! Introduction to WCD Kicks. Sole Kick, Snapping Toe Kick, Cocking Toe Kick, Straight Thrust, Heel Stomp.

ANGULAR CLOSING TECHNIQUES! Single Direct Close, Double Direct Closing, Guy Bo, Hai Bo, Sdp a Step, Steal a Step, Run-Over Close, Shuffle Step, Spring Step on the Half Step, Hart Attack Close, General Comments.

BASIC FORMSa Ging lie, S3 Lum Tao - Exercise Guidelines, Repeated Movements, General Comments, Sil Lum Tao Form, Sil Lum Tao Meditation.

PERSONAL DEVELOPMENT! Becoming an Individual, Personal Communica- tiai. Clarification of a Goal-Growth I^ramid, Game Plan

FOREWORD

The Tao of Wing Chun Do does not advocate violence as a means to settle personal differences. Whenever possible an individual should resolve any potential physical encounter with patience and understanding. He should develop a broad understanding of the futility of trying to adjust conflict through aggressive behavior.

Unfortunately one cannot ignore certain realities of life. There exists throughout the world certain people who do not know how to communicate except by physical means. These individuals, because of their attitude, personal needs and limited emotional maturity, often pose a direct threat to the security and well-being of other individuals.

It is this unfortunate reality which forces the sincere individuals to develop an adequate and controlled method to insure protection of their most basic rights.

The Tao of Wing Chun Do offers a very basic and complete self-protection program. This program is designed for the individual who does not want to become a master, but, m s only the skills needed to defend himself and his family. The Hawaii Martial Arts Academy offers in its Hawaii and Mainland schools the Wing Chun Do system of martial arts. Wing Chun Do is a modern Gung Fu system which complements the Western culture and traditions. By practicing Wing Chun Do, an individual can free himself from many fears and frustrations.

The Wing Chun Do style is a very special martial arts system designed around exact theories and applied principles. To teach this style effectively, the instructor must clearly understand not only the specific principles that make each theory work but he must also be able to present each phase of learning in its proper order. Reading this book or attending one of the training retreats does not qualify a person to teach. If there is anyone in your area who claims to be a Wing Chun Do instructor, please let me know his name and address. I will immediately inform you as to his qualification. Learning from an unqualified instructor will not only limit your ability to his level of incompetence, but will also cause you embarrassment and possible injury if you try to apply your questionable technique.

James W. DeMile

INTRODUCTION

To minimize confusion, the Wing Chun Do program is presented in two volumes. The first volume, in two parts, deals with the basic mental and physical principles that make Wing Chun Do an efficient and practical system. The second volume will cover the more involved knowledge which evolves from the basic principles.

Hopefully the reader will understand the difficulties in learning from a book, and will have the patience to study carefully and clearly this first volume so that he may apply more easily the involved principles in the second volume.

Read the whole book before you begin your program. This will give you an overview of the direction in which you are heading. TTie majority of principles found in Wing Chun Do (as in most martial arts systems) is surprisingly simple. Un; fortunately, many students feel that once they understand a principle, that is sufficient. They quickly become impatient to move on to the next principle. This creates a problem. *Learning* a principle is easy; *training* your body to do a principle is difficult. Your initial reading of the book should give you a general understanding and feeling for the Wing Chun Do principles. All further readings will increase this understanding and offer you a base from which to train.

CHAPTER 1
ORGANIZATION AND STRUCTURE OF A MARTIAL ARTIST

*Anyone can wander through life;
it is the wise man who plans his journey.*

The material in this book is presented as clearly and precisely as possible without becoming philosophical. However, because of the vast amount of material offered, it is necessary that, before beginning to read the next chapters, the student must know what it is he wants to learn. He must develop a base for learning. Most people begin practicing the martial arts without a clear understanding of what will be involved. Therefore, much time and energy is wasted going in the wrong directions.

The base for learning consists of three things:
1. CLARIFICATION OF THE TERM, "MARTIAL ARTIST",
2. A GAUGE (GAME PLAN) TO DETERMINE EVOLUTION OF PROGRESS, and
3. A TRAINING SCHEDULE (To be covered in Chapter 4)

1. CLARIFICATION OF "MARTIAL ARTIST"

The definition of a martial artist varies slightly from student to student. But every definition contains certain basic characteristics. These consistant characteristics will be dealt with here.

To help develop a clear picture of a martial artist, we use a graphic illustration called a Growth Pyramid (Graph 1-A). The use of the Growth Pyramid for general personal development is explained in Part 2. The graph used here is related only to the development of a martial artist.

This pyramid is composed of 14 boxes. The key word to be defined (martial artist, in this case) is put in the largest box (box number 1). In boxes 2 through 13, a quality consistently found in a martial artist is listed. In box 14 is written your goal (success, in this case).

The graph presented here is only a sample. It is to be used as a guide in filling out and using your own graph. At the end of this chapter there is a blank graph. Fill it in with what you consider the important qualities of a martial artist. This enables you to see clearly what will be required of you in order to achieve your goals as a martial artist.

Since only a word or two is being used in each box, elaboration will be necessary in order to establish the exact meaning. In the sample Growth Pyramid a word is used which must be followed up by identifying thoughts that are relative to that particular quality. For example, the word "confidence" is put in box number 2. On a separate sheet of paper, write questions which qualify what confidence means to you. For instance: "Do you have belief in yourself? Do you have faith in your ability?"

After you have written these primary characteristics and your qualifying questions, go back over them. Look at each quality and qualifying question and determine for yourself whether you are weak or strong in that area. To indicate the weak area, put a little star in the comer of that box on the Growth Pyramid. Also put a distinguishing mark on your separate sheet of paper next to the qualifying questions that you feel denote your weak areas. In this way, a glance at your Growth Pyramid will show you generally where improvement is needed, and a glance at your qualifying questions will further pinpoint your weak areas.

Remember, the examples presented in Graph 1 —A are just thoughts to key you to look within yourself and become aware of personal barriers. Each time you eliminate a question or a bit of confusion, more of your energy will be freed to focus on accomplishing your ultimate goals.

Qualifying Questions

Box 2. *Confidence:* Do you believe in yourself? Do you have faith in your abilities? Are you oversensitive to other people's opinions? Do you feel inferior or insecure?

Box 3. *Attitude and Purpose:* Are you patient? Are you open-minded? Are you really willing to train hard? Is it necessary that you must be the best? Are you willing to extend the effort to succeed?

Why are you interested in the martial arts: Because you hope to become a better person? Because you want to earn respect from other people? Because excelling in a martial art will give you a sense of value and pride?

Growth Pyramid
Graph 1—A

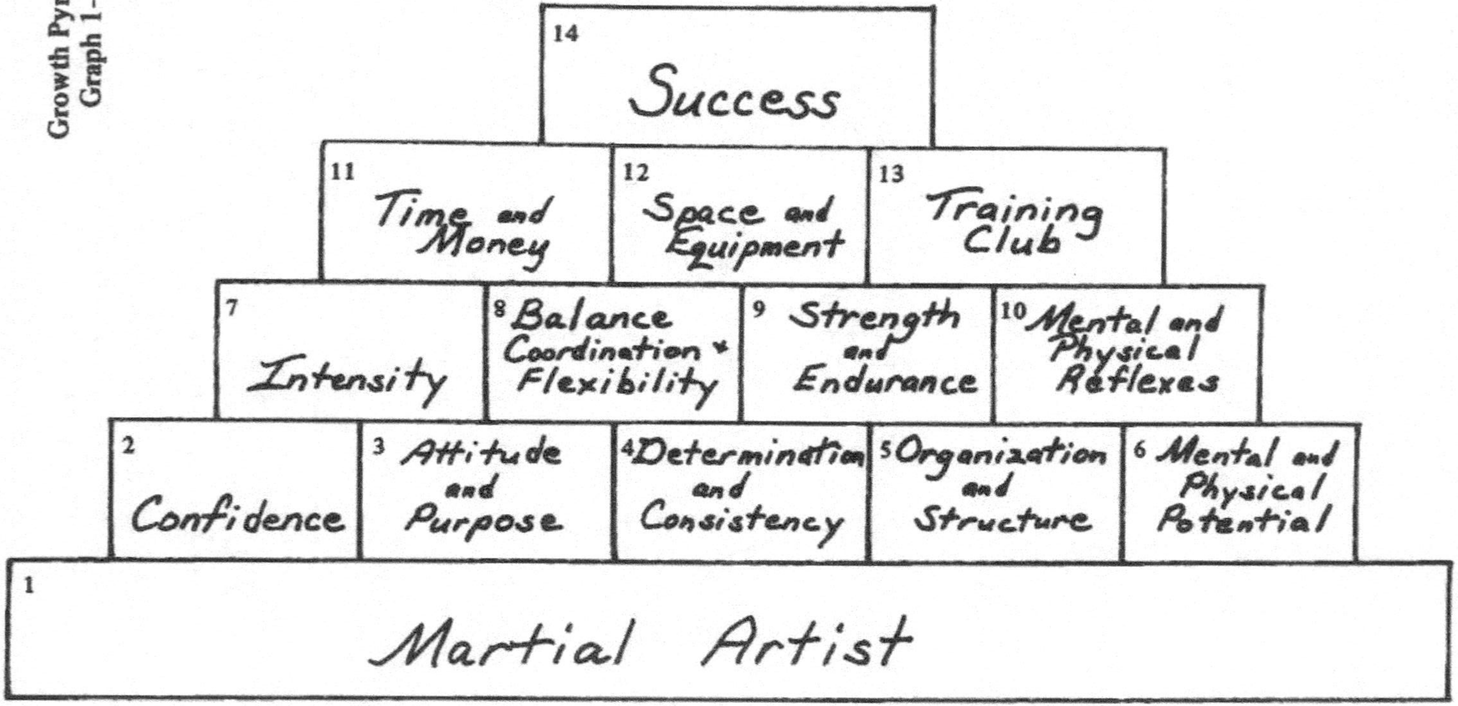

1. Martial Artist
2. Confidence
3. Attitude and Purpose
4. Determination and Consistency
5. Organization and Structure
6. Mental and Physical Potential
7. Intensity
8. Balance, Coordination & Flexibility
9. Strength and Endurance
10. Mental and Physical Reflexes
11. Time and Money
12. Space and Equipment
13. Training Club
14. Success

Box 4. *Determination and Consistency.* Can you follow a schedule? Is it important that you become proficient? Do you follow through on your decisions? Will you train everyday? Are you willing to train for at least one year?

Box 5. *Organization and Structure:* Do you know yourself well enough to establish a training program and follow it through? Can you identify personal areas which need to be developed to become a proficient martial artist? Can you set aside some time each day to practice? Can you project your over-all personal goals so you can determine whether you will be able to stick with a long training program? Can you combine your daily obligations with the responsibilities of time, money and effort needed to become a martial artist?

Box 6. *Mental and Physical Potential'.* Do you have the physical qualities necessary to practice the martial arts? Do you have any handicaps? Is the style you prefer suitable for you? Will it develop your mental needs as well as your physical ones? Do you have lots of fears when you are with aggressive people? Are you afraid of being hurt?

Box 7. *Intensity :* Are you a violent person? Can you control your temper? Do you ever "explode" for no apparent reason? Do you dislike violence? Are you willing to practice contact sparring?

Box 8. *Balance, Coordination and Flexibility :* Are you a relaxed person? D) you move with a natural flow? Are you agile? How is your eye-hand coordination? Can you maintain balance on one foot? Can you touch your toes without bending your knees? Is your spine stiff or loose? Do you feel awkward? Can you kick as high as your head? Do you excel in any sport?

Box 9. *Strength and Endurance:* Do you feel healthy? Do you "bum out" easily? Are you strong for your body size? Can you run 2 miles? Are your muscles firm or spongy? Do your muscles ache after a little exercise?

Box 10. *Mental and Physical Reflexes^* Do you respond quickly to surprise situations? Do you get confused easily? Do you tense up when reacting quickly under pressure? Can you see fine movement easily? Do you have broad peripheral vision? Are you a spontaneous person?

Box 11. *Time and Money :* Do you have enough free time to practice the martial arts? Do you have enough time to achieve your goal? Is your time schedule flexible so you can change your training schedule as needed? Will you be able to attend 90% of all training sessions? Can you afford to practice? Can you purchase the equipment necessary to set up a well-rounded home program?

Box 12. *Space and Equipment:* Do you have adequate training space in your home? Can you get the equipment needed for home training, which will fit well into your space?

Box 13. *Training Club'.* Does the club offer the style in which you are interested? Is the instructor qualified? Is the instructor mature or on an "ego trip"? Will your instructor answer your questions? Does the instructor help those who are having difficulties? Does the club have a comfortable feeling about it? Do the students seem relaxed and positive about their club? Does the club have rules? Are the students really required to follow these rules? Is any dangerous horseplay allowed? Does the club have sufficient training equipment? Does the instructor show an interest in your health and wellbeing? Are you asked to sign a contract? Can you leave the club without any financial penalties? Is the club close enough to allow regular practice?

Box 14. *Success:* Are you willing to develop in all the areas specified in this graph? Are you honestly willing to do your best to become a well-developed, mature martial artist? *Then do it!*

2. GAME PLAN

The Growth Pyramid establishes your weak areas. The Game Plan is an organized and structured method of working on these weak areas.

The use of the Game Plan for general personal development is explained in Part 2. Hie plan used here is related only to the development of a martial artist.

Refer to Game Plan, Graph 2—A. Remember this is only a sample.

A. Put down your name, age and that day's date.

B. Primary Goal: Write in the key word or words (found in your box number 1 in your Growth Pyramid).

C. Secondary Goals: List 4 qualities from your Pyramid that are weak areas needing immediate attention (the ones you have starred).

D. **Things to Accomplish This Month:** Fill in all eight blanks (if possible) with specific efforts you can make to eliminate some of the problems you have noted in (C). Be honest and write only those things you will actually try to accomplish within that month.

E. Daily Goal Progression: The numbers 1 to 31 under the graph denote the days of the month. The numbers 0 to 10 on the left side of the graph denote your grading system. Number 0 denotes knowing nothing. The numbers from 1 to 5 show that a little effort to a reasonable amount of effort has been exerted. Those from 6 to 10 show a considerable to a very great effort. Number 10 indicates an almost fanatical effort.

At the end of each day evaluate (0 to 10) the efforts you made to accomplish any pf the assignments in (D). Be fair; if you have not done anything, mark an X in zero. If you have tried to work on something, you may put an X in 2. If you have extended genuine effort to improve through reading, practice or discussion, you may score yourself 6 or 7. Of course, the higher the score the more effort you must exert. Mark your chart daily so that you can graphically see the amount of consistent effort you used during the month.

Comments

Several important points must be emphasized regarding this Game Plan. It is designed so that you must use the entire plan (A through E) to achieve maximum benefit.

It is *your* Game Plan. Everything you put down in B, C and D is important in your development. Hopefully, writing down these selected areas of importance will stimulate you to work on them.

This Game Plan should be used for at least three consecutive months. By that time you will have established a natural tendency to stay organized. When you become organized and can define specific problems, then it will be much easier for you to plan the means to overcome these problems.

GAME PLAN
Graph 2-A

(A) NAME.................................. AGE .... DATE...............

(B) PRIMARY GOAL....................

(C) SECONDARY GOALS (in order of importance)

    1..

    2..

    3..

    4..

(D) THINGS TO ACCOMPLISH THIS MONTH (in order of importance)

    1................................. 5....................................

    2................................. 6....................................

    3................................. 7....................................

    4................................. 8....................................

(E)   **DAILY GOAL PROGRESSION**

Growth Pyramid

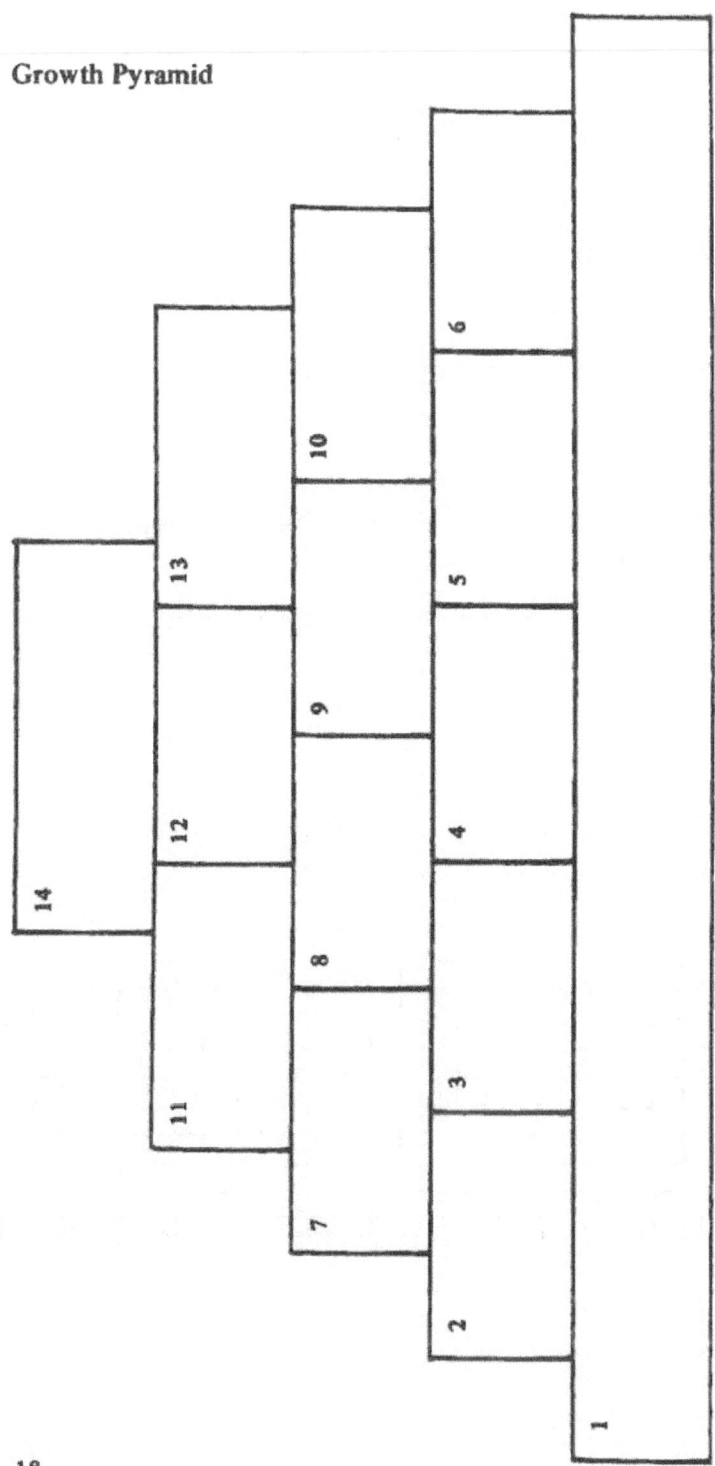

GAME PLAN

NAME.................................. AGE.............. DATE...............

PRIMARY GOAL ....

SECONDARY GOALS (in order of importance)

    1 ....

    2 ....

    3 ....

    4 ....

THINGS TO ACCOMPLISH THIS MONTH (in order of importance)

1.. 5......................................

2.. 6......................................

3.. 7... ....

4.. 8.... . ...

DAILY GOAL PROGRESSION

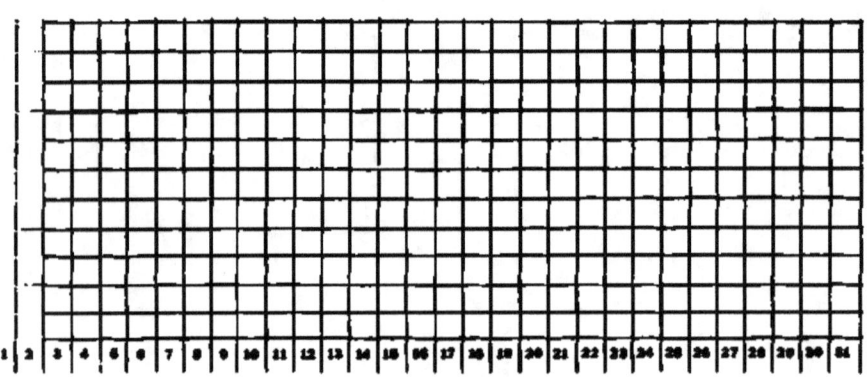

QUESTIONS - ORGANIZATION AND STRUCTURE OF A MARTIAL ARTIST

1. What makes up a base for learning?
2. In Chapter 1, what is the purpose of the Growth Pyramid?
3. Define in less than 100 words what a martial artist is.
4. What is a Game Plan?
5. What is the purpose of a daily goal progression?
6. What is your goal as a martial artist?

CHAPTER 2
BREATHING AND MEDITATION

Proper breathing techniques eliminate many of the internal barriers that create tension and restrict movements. Correct breathing feeds fresh oxygen into one's entire system, keeping it alive, alert and responsive.

Specific meditation techniques clear the mind of distractions and restrictive fears. They stabilize the emotions for harmonbous internal flow. They create a firm base for more dynamic expression of technique, power and speed.

BREATHING

The act of proper breathing brings fresh oxygeh to one's lungs and opens a reservoir of energy. Unfortunately, because of improper methods of and attitudes towards walking, standing and sitting, most people breathe with only one-third of their total lung capacity. The simple, natural act of breathing revitalizes the total body. As we breathe deeply, we increase the supply of oxygen into the bloodstream and hence into the muscles, joints and organs of the body.

To relearn the natural act of deep breathing, it is necessary, first of all, that you are relaxed. In any situation where you are tense or out-o^reath, do not attempt to learn correct breathing.

SAVASANA
This is a yoga pose for relaxation.
Lie on your back, arms a few inches from your body.
Place palms up so that your energy is free to flow out into the universe. Spread your legs comfortably apart. Feel that your spine is in line. Drop your shoulders down slightly; keep your chin tucked in. Close your eyes; concentrate inward. Keep your mind and body relaxed. Breathe slowly and regulariy.

COMPLETE BREATH
Once you feel relaxed, inhale deeply through the nose. The nose is a natural filter which cleans and warms

the incoming air. Let the abdomen relax and balloon out as the diaphragm relaxes and falls against it. Air fills first the lower, then the middle and finally the top of the lungs.

Hold the breath a couple of seconds.

Exhale slowly through the nose, drawing the abdomen in and then lifting it up slightly as the last bit of air leaves.

At first the inhaling, holding and exhaling should take about 10 seconds. It should be one continuous flowing act. Once the move becomes more natural, the time can be lengthened.

It is important that you inhale slowly, completely filling lower, middle and upper lungs. It is also necessary to exhale completely. If all the stale air is not removed, the fresh supply of oxygen will not be totally used. But if you exhale completely, driving out all the stale air, the fresh oxygen will be able to fill the lungs, thus sending into the blood stream the oxygen necessary for total revitalization.

Two other breathing exercises are given here. Once you have practiced the basic moves of all three breathing patterns, they may be used singly, mixed (e.g. 5 complete breaths, a cleansing breath, 5 complete breaths, etc.) or in conjunction with stretching and other exercises.

CLEANSING BREATH

The cleansing breath shows more dramatically the benefits of complete, correct breathing.

Inhale, as in the complete breath. Retain the breath for a couple of seconds. Pucker the lips as if for a whistle, but do not swell out the cheeks. Exhale, blowing out with considerable pressure until every bit of breath is gone. Simultaneously, suck the stomach in hard, pressing air out from below. Muscles should contract like a tube of toothpaste being rolled neatly from the bottom.

VITAUC BREATH

The vitalic breath strengthens and completely clears out the lungs.

Breathe in through the nose in a series of sharp sniffs until your lungs are completely filled. Hold a couple of seconds. Then blow out explosively through the mouth with a sound like a loudly whispered "haaa" •

Do not dwell on the breathing exercises. Relax; concentrate only on your breath; practice the breathing pattern and then move on to something else. After a short time you will notice that during the day you will be taking complete breaths more often.

MEDITATION - A PILGRIMAGE WITHIN

Meditation is a mysterious word that has countless meanings. Yet in spite of these various meanings all meditation has a common purpose - to allow the individual to journey within himself.

This chapter does not deal with the techniques used to overcome everyday personal problems. These will be covered in Part 2. This chapter concentrates on simple methods to create a stable mental-physical base from *which* one's martial arts potential can evolve.

There are two types of meditation — indirect and direct.

INDIRECT MEDITATION

Indirect meditation is the process of detaching or withdrawing from daily responsibilities by eliminating conventional conscious thinking. This is done by concentrating on a specific reference point or word. This indirect approach dissolves much of the tension and stress which restrict daily growth.

Underlying the indirect approach is the belief that each individual has an innate ability to resolve conflicts and stimulate positive expansion. This ability does not function well if the conscious is hampered by emotional troubles and turmoil. Consciously focusing on a neutral thought or spot rids the conscious of much of this emotional restraint. The subconscious then is free to use its natural, unlimited potential to develop the total person.

DIRECT MEDITATION

Direct meditation brings together the potential of both your conscious and subconscious. This is done through the process of structured developmental suggestion and specific imagery techniques.

The indirect method uses the conscious mind to free the subconscious so the individual is helped; the direct method uses positive $ jggestion to free both the conscious and subconscious in order to aid the individual.

The indirect approach allows the river to flow under the direction of nature, whereas the direct approach narrows and directs the river's energy source into specific channels so the maximum results can be achieved with a minimum of effort and time.

FIRST STEP - THE KEY WORD

The first step in any meditation is to establish a point of reference at which the inward journey begins. Too often, circumstances do not permit an easy inner withdrawal because the conscious is distracted by surrounding influences or personal conflicts that restrict concentration. To minimize these disruptive influences, a key word will be used to establish a conditioned response between the conscious and subconscious.

This conditioned response acts to immediately dissolve internal and surrounding diversions so the conscious can come into harmony with the subconscious.

Key Word Exercise

First, the key word must be established. Your name is usually the best word to use. You can use your first or last name, or even a nickname. Your conscious and subconscious identify peisonally with your name and can easily respond without possible conflict. Once you have determined the word you will use, you are ready to begin the exercise.

This exercise is only a sample guide to be used at your own discretion. When verbalizing to yourself, do it quietly in your own mind — the conscious speaks to the subconscious. Read this exercise a number of times and practice until you develop a smooth flow of thoughts.

Isolate yourself where you will not be disturbed for at least 15 minutes. Take care of any basic needs that might prove distracting such as hunger, thirst or the restroom.

Darken the room to minimize visual distractions. Once you are ready to begin, loosen any tight clothing. Lie on a soft surface in a comfortable position. Try to equalize body pressure so you are not really aware of any one part (e.g. Do not cross one leg over the other or cross your hands on your chest.). If at any time during this exercise you wish to move or change position, do so; but move slowly so that a comfortable feeling is maintained.

Close your eyes. Imagine you are looking into space. There are no stars or lights — just a beautiful, peaceful emptiness. In a moment you are going to step through the doorway of your mind into that emptiness — just freeing yourself from all worldly problems ... all your fears, frustrations and tensions • • • enjoying a tranquil, warm, pleasant feeling as you drift deeper into that endless mental void. You know that at anytime you wish you can end it by simply opening your eyes. Until you open your eyes, however, you will just "let go" more and more as you become more and more relaxed.

Take 3 deep breaths. As you exhale on the third one, imagine yourself "letting go; ' as if riding a magic carpet through that doorway and out into that secure inner world which is yours. As you drift, focus on freeing your body from any muscle tension. Starting at the head, imagine all the facial muscles becoming loose and limp. Slowly move through the body, pushing off any tension — dissolve any tightness as if you were pressing it down and out your feet. Feel the lightness fill the body as the muscles relax. A wave of relaxation spreads down over the head, through the body and out the feet.

Keep your eyes closed at all times and let your breathing settle to a deep, regular rhythm. Once your body is relaxed, you should begin, mentally, to give soft, relaxing suggestions.

"I am completely 'letting go'. • • relaxing every muscle • • • every nerve ... every fiber in my body. As I relax, I will have no disturbances or distractions. I will free myself from all mental and physical tensions and enjoy this beautiful, quiet peaceful feeling. As I relax more, I will detach more from all my daily conflicts . .. This will allow me to completely rest my mind and body."

At this point, you should slowly drift and enjoy the

emptiness that is filling your body. Do not be in a hurry; just completely "let go" • To help you relax even more, use lazy, peaceful words. As you are thinking these gentle throughts of relaxation place your key word into the subconscious.

"I am completely relaxed . ... My mind and body are enjoying this calm, tranquil feeling. I am at peace with myself ... My mind and body are one, sensitive and responsive to my suggestions. I am pleased with this sense of well-being. I will be able to easily return to this state whenever I consciously wish by using my key word

." (Say your key word.)^sAfter I use my key word, no matter where I am or how I feel, I will be able to clear my mind • • • dissolve all tension ... and respond to my suggestions?*

Reinforcement of the key word should take place before you finish this exercise.

"Each time I use my key word I will

respond better. I will be able to just 'let go' and eiyoy the calmness that fills my mind and body. I will be the complete master of myself and be able to give myself positive suggestions and follow them carefully. I will be able to expand all my mental-physical potential without any conscious or subconscious resistance. My key word will be like a magic wand freeing me from tension and allowing me to concentrate on my immediate concerns.

Now in a moment I am going to slowly count from 1 to 5. At the count of 5 I will open my eyes, feeling refreshed • • • alert... and responsive to my suggestions. Each and every time I practice, I will do better... concentrate more • • • and relax ... no matter how tense or nervous I am. I will always respond to my key word without any effort ... and will always look forward to this inner communication that frees me to achieve my potential, and my personal goals." (Slowly count from i to 5.) "1 • • • 2 • • • 3 • • • 4 • • •

This is not conventional hypnosis. You will not be in a trance. All that will happen is that you will simply withdraw for a minute from all of your personal tensions, conflicts and frustrations. During this withdrawal you will be able to rest your mind and body and, through the use of direct personal suggestions, eliminate many negative qualities which have been restricting your mental-physical growth. This chapter deals only with your martial arts capabilities.

Comments

Practice this exercise once a day for a week. Once you have firmly established your key word in the subconscious, there is no need for further reinforcement. You can expand your practice to applications of the key word.

Initially the key word will be used to help you "let go" when you meditate. However, you will quickly find that your key word is not limited to meditation. If you feel tense or anxious, just close your eyes for a moment and repeat your key word. The tightness and conflict will dissolve like sugar in water so you can clearly approach the problem and eliminate it.

At this point it should be clarified that if you wish to "let go" and become really relaxed you will be able to do so providing you are in an appropriate situation. If you are driving a car and use your key, you will just relax but not with any loss of driving control. If you are in a situation where you must stay alert both mentally and physically such as when participating in a sporting event, then you will pair your key word with positive suggestions about concentration, energetic feeling and an alert mind. Much of your response, when you use the key word, will depend on what you want to accomplish. You cannot hurt yourself. If you should accidentally give a negative suggestion, the subconscious will just reject it.

CONTROL AND DIRECTION OF YOUR BREATHING

Meditation is a refined art of concentration that demands a high degree of inner breath and thought control.

Exercise 1

First, close your eyes. Imagine all the muscular power in your body turning into an explosive electrical energy that vibrates and flows throughout your whole system. Feel the muscles twitch as this dynamic current of power.pulsates with a building intensity.

Spend as much time as necessary to develop and recognize this awesome force. It is important that you are able to excite this volatile strength as an instinctive response.

Once you have changed body power into an active, visual energy source, turn to your breathing.

Exercise 2

Sit or lie with eyes closed. Draw in a slow, complete breath through the nose. As you inhale imagine that your breath is a warm fluid that is drawn down, not only into your lungs, but throughout your body. As this life source spreads into every segment of your being, it begins to blend with the electro-muscular energy. It acts as a catalyst to magnify your power potential so that you begin to feel an overwhelming sense of strength. Imagine this energy as being so explosive that you could strike through walls, smash bricks and bend steel.

As you exhale, puise your lips together and allow this dynamic force to flow — like molten lava streams out and drains your body, leaving you with an empty, hollow, peaceful feeling. Then repeat this process.

After you become comfortable with this total integration of mind-body power you will refine it, so it becomes a controlled energy source to direct and explode whenever you wish.

Exercise 3

Instead of allowing the mind-body power to flow out when you exhale, lock it in. Only residual waste that has been strained of its vital life force will be exhaled.

Let your breathing pattern become deep and regular. Focus all your attention on moving this flowing energy into various parts of the body. As you inhale, see this explosive life force filling your right leg while leaving the rest of the body hollow and empty. Feel the right leg tighten as the power tries to escape from that tight space. Hold the strength in the leg as you exhale. As you inhale move the energy to the left leg. Try at all times to see this energy as a life flowing mass of power that only goes where you direct it.

Do this same exercise directing the energy throughout the rest of the body, even the head.

Exercise 4

When you have learned to channel your mental energies easily and control the movement of the physical energies, then extend your right arm out straight with the hand open and the fingeis pointing forward. Bring the energy up into the right arm and as you exhale slowly through pursed lips, imagine that the energy is also streaming out your finger tips in a solid flow of power that could burn holes through steel. Periodically stop exhaling and force more energy out the finger tips. You should actually be able to feel an increase of power flow. You can move this energy into other parts of the body and let it flow from any chosen source* You may change the position of your fingers so the energy flows at angles or you can also close the hand into a fist and allow the power to rush out the fist like water from a dam that has burst.

******

The energy developed by these four mindbody exercises is referred to as "Concentrated Energy Flow".

POWER MEDITATION
Sil Lim Tao

The Sil Um Tao is a basic form that is presented in Part 2. Hie application both as an exercise and power meditation will be coveted at that time.

Bamboo Meditation

In Hawaii, this was a popular meditation because bamboo was easily accessible. 'Unfortunately, it is difficult for most people to acquire the necessary amount and type of bamboo. We will retain the name "Bamboo Meditation", but the use of a rubber inner tube will be supplemented. This meditation is done for only one minute. If you are doing it correctly, you will not be able to do it for any longer.

Equipment Needed

Take a used inner tube — preferably one that would fit a large American car. Cut a 2 inch wide strip from the tube. Be sure not to have any cuts or holes in the section you select as it may suddenly break and cause you to pull a muscle.

Beginning Position

Stand with your right foot forward about 8 inches from the left. Stand fairly erect; do not lean backwards. Place the inner tube section on your wrists and extend your arms out in front of you with elbows about 3 inches from your body (2—1). Your palms will be open and facing upward (2—2). Use your key word, relax, clear your mind. You may close your eyes to accentuate the inner focus.

Exercise for Lines of Energy Flow

Inhale, allowing your concentrated energy flow to move up into both arms. As you slowly exhale, you will begin to move your arms forward and outward against the rubber (2—3). You should time your breath so you have fully exhaled when you reach full extension. Magnify your concentrated energy flow as the arms are projected. See the power streaming out the finger tips of both hands. Move the arms outward and forward as much as you can. Then as you inhale) *slowly* allow the arms to return to their original position and begin again. Do not rest or pause between motions. *Do not allow the arms 纪 spring in after the full extension.* Just slowly allow them to return to the beginning position. The amount of extensions will depend on your breathing pattern. Do not think of how many or how well you are doing. Concentrate on projecting your total being through the arms and out the hands.

This meditation should be done 3 times a day. First, at the wrist, then at the elbows (2—4 and 5) and then over the palms (2—6 and 7). The energy flow is the same for all three. Each one affects different muscle plexus and has varying degrees of difficulty. All three should be

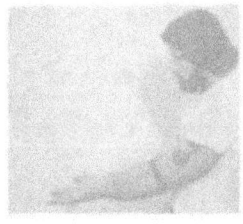

2-1

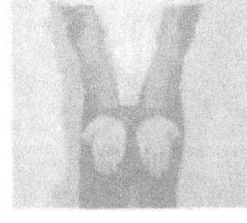

2-2

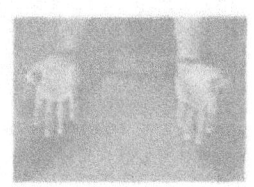

2-3

done with the same angles of energy flow and the same focused concentration. Do not maintain any position for more than one minute.

When you feel adequate progress has been made, you can take a 3 inch strip of tube and continue your exercise. 4 inches would be the last phase. Then you can return to the 2 inch strip and do the exercise for 2 minutes at a time. You should not try to progress from one phase td another in less than 30 days.

Comments

This is primarily for power development. Most of your technique in this system will call for springy flowing energy from the upper torso. A natural by-product of this exercise is the tendency to direct your energy forward into the opponent.

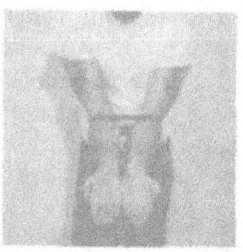

2–4

2-5

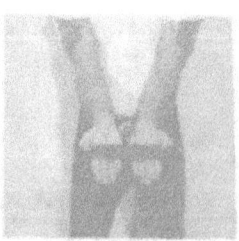

2-6

2-7

PAPER MEDITATION - A SOFT POWER EXERCISE

The use of energy in this exercise will be a subdued form of the concentrated energy flow. In this exercise, you will have the same mind-body energy except that you have tamed it so it will flow like a peaceful river, a river that appears gentle on the surface but is in reality a storehouse of explosive power ready to overcome anything that tries to stop it.

Equipment Needed

A smooth-surfaced table that is no higher than the navel area (2-8). A straight-backed chair and a sheet of paper, 8/ by 11 inches. A quiet semiilit room with adequate ventilation is best. Wear loose, comfortable clothing.

Ready Position

Sit upright in the chair, your body about 3 inches from the table. Take the paper and crumple it into a tight ball (2—9). Then open the crumpled ball. Lay it flat on the table with the long way to the right and left, and centered to you (2—10). The distance of the paper away from you will depend on your reach. You should be able to reach the upper edge without straining or leaning forward. The inner edge should be no closer than 1 inch from the edge of the table closest to you.

2-8

2-9

2—10

2-11

2—12

2—13

2-14

Exercise

The purpose of this exercise is to eliminate in one sitting as many wrinkles in the paper as you can.

Use your key word to clear your mind and begin to feel the mind-body energy moving into both arms. Lean your head slightly forward and concentrate on a point 1 inch above the center of the paper. You will maintain that visual point at all times. Place your hands in a prayer position about 3 inches over the center of the paper (2—11). In one continuous motion slowly exhale and let your energy flow through the edge of your hands to the paper; lower your hands to the paper and press down firmly (not hard) with the edge of your hands (2-12). Immediately begin to spread the hands apart so as the lower edges move out, the thumbs, staying together will lower side by side until both hands, still pressing firmly, are flat on the paper (2—13). Continuing to the right and left, both hands will pull away from one another smoothing the paper as they move outward. As the outer edge of the hands reach the edge of the paper, they will lift slightly as the rest of the hand continues to smooth the paper. As the thumbs reach the edge, both hands will lift slightly (2—14) and return to the original prayer position.

Exhale as soon as you begin to drop the hands towards the paper. You should finish exhaling as your thumbs lift from the paper. Inhale as the hands raise back into the starting position. See the flow of energy as a sweeping action that pushes away each wrinkle. Maintain a constant speed and pressure.

Comments

This simple meditation exercise will develop an unbelieve- able sweeping energy throughout your upper torso. This is soft power — dynaixiic strength hidden under the cloak of simple movement. A by-product of this exercise is tremendous patience. If you can straighten every wrinkle out of that paper in one sitting you are a very patient person.

MEDITATION FOR SPEED

Primarily this exercise helps develop your reactions and your speed of motion. It may be practiced using either hand strikes or kicks. No power will be used in this exercise since

you will be striking only at air.
Equipment Needed
A television in working condition.
Beginning Position
Place the TV about 8 feet in front of you. It can be at any height — even on the floor, as long as you can see it clearly at all times. Turn on a program that has a lot of action. Switch the channel, if you find the pictures do not change much. (A talk show is usually poor; a cartoon or a fast-paced program is good.) *Do " of turn up the sound: use the picture only.*

Wear loose, comfortable clothing. You may be barefooted or wear athletic shoes. Your mind will be relaxed and your body will be loose and springy. Use your key word. Think to yourself — "I am going to be loose at all times, springy, light and flexible. I will concentrate only on the exercise and not be bothered by disturbances or distractions. My body action will be smooth and controlled. All my strikes will be snappy and precise."
Exercise
Stand in an upright position with your feet a little less than shoulder width. Keep your elbows at your sides. Place your hands in front of you, palms together (2—15). Begin to move your hands together just as if they were all covered with grime and you wanted to remove it all. They will touch at all times when not striking, and maintain this constant washing motion. Once you begin the hand motion, continue it until you complete the exercise.

2-15

2-16

2-17

The TV picture will be constantly changing from one scene to another. Every time the picture shifts to another scene, you will punch (2—16) or kick, immediately recover your position and continue to wash the hands (2—17). Your striking action can be either a straight punch at the TV or a kick of your choice. Remember, *no* povvez Snap your strike, but be cautious of the elbow and knee joints. You must strike everytime the picture changes; you cannot just strike when you want. Keep your mind clear, your body relaxed and your movement smooth.

Although you start from a stationary position, as you do the exercise, it is permissible to move slightly to the right or left, and even forward and backward like a boxer. You must stay in front of the TV and watch it at all times.

Do this exercise as long as you can maintain the constant reaction to the scene changing. If you begin to skip a lot or get tired and sloppy, stop doing the exercise.

Comments

This is a beautiful exercise to develop quick reflexes and a smooth, snappy motion. This technique was learned from Mike Lee of Seattle, Washington, who also studied under Bruce Lee. Mike said that after he practiced this exercise for a while he found it difficult to just reach for something without snapping out with a strike. He knocked over a lot of glasses before he learned to refine his reactions!

This exercise is good for focusing on a point while in motion. It tends to help you disperse your vision (where you see what you are looking at, but are not aware of details). Your peripheral visual focus is sharpened by this exercise because you must make a conscious effort not to watch the actual TV program.

IMAGERY MEDITATION

This meditation develops technique, speed and coordination. It is presented here as a general exercise for using your mental potential to accelerate the learning process. Once you have finished reading this book, you will find this meditation extremely beneficial in your learning of technique.

This is a stationary meditation technique; it uses your imagination like a TV screen on which you can project specific exercises. It should be done in a quiet atmosphere where you will not be disturbed for at least 30 minutes.

The principle of this exercise is to withdraw into the inner conscious and establish a perfect training area where you can be both participant and observer. It will be necessary to outline specific areas oh which you would like to work. The example presented here is only to give you an idea of how the imagery meditation may be applied.

Example of Imagery Meditation

Ready Position

Lie on your back on a bed in a darkened room with no disturbances. Loosen clothing. Eyes are closed and the key word is used to clear your mind of the day's events and to free the body of distracting tension. Your breathing will settle into a regular pattern.

Placing of Suggestions

After the key word, give a few simple directive suggestions such as: "I am going to just relax without any disturbances or distractions. I am going to soon fill my mind with thoughts of watching myself practicing evasive weaving. I will work out first against a boxer, then in succession against a karate man, a street fighter and a 2 man attack. I will not use offensive technique at first, only defensive techniques that will allow me to slip my opponent's attacks. I will be loose and move with a calm quickness. I will move on the balls of my feet, keeping my knees slightly bent at all times, so as to insure a springy motion My footwork will be precise and coordinated well with body action. When I begin to add offensive techniques, they will blend in well with my body motion and the offensive moves of my opponent. I will always stress simplicity, efficiency and practicality in all my moves. As I do this mentd meditation, my body will learn from this experience as if I was really doing it. In that way I can develop my own natural ability to maintain mind-body control"

The above suggestions have been rather precise. This is so you can fully concentrate on your mental images without having to stop and interfere.

Mental Exercise

Allow yourself at least 15 minutes to fill your mind with all the images you have projected. Focus completely on the principles and techniques that you have outlined. Your exercise will be like a daydream; eliminate all outside disturbances and distractions so that you can concentrate completely on it.

Comments

Katas or a particular technique may be practiced. You can add speed to your motion once the basic moves and principles are learned.

Practice simple techniques at first. Spend time being an observer and then switch to a participant role.

More concentration and clarity will be developed as you practice imagery. In time, the body will actually be able to learn the action as if you were physically doing it.

CANDLE MEDITATION

The candle meditation develops visual focus and internal energy flow. It is a soft stationary meditation.

Equipment Needed

A candle that will burn for at least 30 minutes, and a candle holder. A room that can be isolated from outside light and drafts. A table to hold the candle.

Beginning Position

Eliminate any possible drafts (from under doors, windows, etc.). Place the candle holder with candle in the center of the table and light it. The candle should be a little lower than eye level. When lit the flame should stand straight up without wavering.

Exercise

Sit in a comfortable position. You will need to be at ease for at least 30 minutes. You should be 2 to 3 feet away from the candle with the flame clearly visible at all times. Use your key word and give directive suggestions.

"I will eliminate all mental disturbances and distractions and focus all my thoughts and physical powers out of my eyes and into the base of the candle flame. I will channel all my mind-body energy with such force that I will be able to make the flame move and dance about at will. The longer I do this the stronger my energy flow will become so at some given point, I could push over the candle with my intensity."

Comments

This is a simple meditation but the results are profound.

You will experience a heightened awareness of everything that is about you. You will know without doubt that, at will, you can project the energy from your body and direct it to any specific target.

VASE MEDITATION

The vase meditation lowers your center of balance and creates a low axis for stable motion.

Exercise

Sit on the floor or on a chair or stand. Keep your back and head erect. Use your key word, relax; dissolve mental-physical distractions.

Close your eyes. Imagine there is a long-necked vase that goes from the top of your throat to your navel area (Note drawing).

Inhale through your nose. Visualize the incoming breath moving down the neck of the vase to the bottom, and then making two small circular actions. See and feel the warm air creating a slight pressure against the bottom of the vase as it circles. When the circular action is complete, exhale. The breath will move back up the neck of the vase and out your mouth through pursed lips. The exhalation will continue until the air is completely out of the vase. Continue this breathing action for 5 minutes.

Comments

Your total mental energy should be focused on seeing and feeling the breath in motion. After a while you will actually experience a warm, settled feeling in the pit of your stomach. You will feel a distinct lowered center of gravity as you move through technique. This exercise should be emphasized when doing the closed Bi Jong exercises (Chapter 6).

COMPLEMENTARY EXERCISES

The following exercises are given to help develop more body awareness for meditation.

Blindfold Exercises

This should be done in your home or in a familiar and secure environment. You should allow 2 hours for this exercise. *Exercise*

Completely blindfold your eyes so there is no visual stimulation. Without removing the blindfold for any reason, go about your normal activity. Try not to stay in one spot too long. Establish a number of things to do which will require coordinated body movement. As you move about, try to visualize the space in which you are moving. See the room with your mind's eye. Become aware of each move and action of the body. It will be as if you can see inside your whole body and are personally responsible for every effort to move.

Comments

This exercise will make you very sensitive and aware of total body action. It will sensitize the mental awareness of your body in motion. After doing this exercise a few times you will develop a much closer feeling for your body and its function. This will help you when stretching, doing station training or practicing basic technique.

Single Arm Exercise

This exercise develops independence of single limb action. It expands control and use of the limbs. It is to be done for one complete day from the time you arise until you return to bed at night.

Exercise

Immediately when rising in the morning, tape, tie or strap your primary arm to your side. If you are righthanded that would be your primary arm. Spend the whole day with this arm strapped to your side. Do not avoid normal activities. When using the free hand, try to become more aware of its total movement. Appreciate its freedom by trying to use it as much as possible throughout the day.

Comments

This type of exercise will allow you to appreciate the uniqueness of the arm's ability, and to respect the potential of both arms working together but remaining independent.

This exercise can also be done with the other arm or one of the legs. You would have to get a pair of crutches or a wheel chair for the leg exercise.

******

Because of the effort needed at first to learn these meditation exercises, you may prefer to schedule them at a different time from your regular workout (perhaps early morning or late evening). This will allow you to totally concentrate on the meditation exercises and give you more time for your regular workout. Once the meditation exercises are clear to you they may be scheduled as part of your regular workout.

A basic use of your key word when starting will be enough to help you relax and prepare yourself for training.

Two of the meditations will be used quite often in the power exercises since they complement that level of training. The principles of bamboo meditation will be found in the physical exercise, double Doan Chi. TV meditation will be used as a soft exercise to develop reflexes.

QUESTIONS - BREATHING AND MEDITATION
1. Why is proper breathing important?
2. Name 3 breathing techniques.
3. What is meant by stale air?
4. What is the first step necessary in order to learn the complete breath?
5. What is the difference between direct and indirect meditation?
6. What is a common root of all meditation?
7. What is a key word?
8. Name 3 uses for the key word.
9. Explain how you develop concentrated energy flow.
10. What is the purpose of bamboo meditation?
11. What does paper meditation develop?
12. What is the procedure for doing TV meditation?
13. Give 2 reasons for imagery meditation.
14. How is your energy focus helped by candle meditation?
15. Describe the vase meditation and its benefits.
16. Why should a person do the blindfold exercise?

CHAPTER 3
STRETCHING

Stretching allows the individual to develop the flexibility and muscle tone necessary for speed, coordination and spring power.

STRETCHING

General health and physical fitness are dependent on several factors. A person has no control over the factors determined by heredity and health status, but working within his capacity he determines his general physical fitness by how he fills his basic needs. These basic needs are exercise, sleep, proper breathing, wholesome diet, proper thinking and con- centration of the mind.

The stretching program offered here is not a comprehensive one. It is merely one small step towards the fulfillment of the body's need for exercise. These stretching positions are shown because they complement the techniques and principles offered in this book. They also develop general awareness of your body.

Stretching loosens your muscles. Minimize all resistance so the muscle is free to expand. If the muscle is to be developed rather than stretched, resistance must be placed against that muscle. This resistance can be either isometric or physical (such as in Power Exercises, Chapter 4).

Work for total flexibility. In Wing Chun Do, the body works as a single unit so that all muscle groups must be able to function singly, together or rapidly one after another. If one body part is not flexible enough, another part of the body must follow up with a different technique rather than the one which would have come naturally for a totally flexible person. This, of course, means the technique will be slower and probably not as effective as the natural move would have been.

Do every stretching exercise according to your limitations. You are working with your body, not someone else's, so do not try to do what another person is doing. Do not criticize your body; just observe it and work with it. From day to day, morning to night, you will notice differences in it.

Accept these differences. Take pleasure in the exercises you do well and be patient with those you do poorly. Develop a well-rounded program containing both.

It is the method of doing the exercise that is important. The type of stretches you do will be determined by the type of activity you are going to do.

Never tug, strain, bounce or pull strenuously. Forcing will tend to cause your body to resist and actually slow down your progression. Do not rush through any exercise. It is better to do an exercise once, slowly stretching and holding at each position, than to rush through it a number of times. The number of times an exercise should be done will depend on the individual. An out-of-condition person may benefit more from doing an exercise once, than a conditioned person would repeating it 20 times. The number given at the end of each exercise is to be used simply as a guide.

Some stretches require that you hold a position. On these, stretch until you "feel it" and hold. Then do not move, squirm or fidget. Relax, breathe deeply and regularly. As you hold your position, completely relaxing, you probably will become aware that you do not "feel it" anymore and will have to stretch a little more to "feel it" again. Hold each position a minumum of 60 seconds. Come out of the stretch slowly.

These stretches are given in no particular order. After deciding which part of your body needs stretching, choose which exercises to do.

3-1

3-2

3—3

FOUR-WAY STRETCH

1. Stand with feet together, hands at your sides. Inhale deeply and raise arms overhead. Interlock fingers, palms up. (Fingers stay interlocked throughout the entire exercise.) Hold breath and stretch upward on tiptoes (3—1).
2. Exhale, lower heels, and bend forward, touching the floor, if possible, with clasped hands. Bring hands close to feet, or as far down as you can. Keep knees straight (3-2).
3. Inhale and come up to standing position with arms raised, elbows straight. Hold breath. Bend to the left and to the right (3—3) without bending your elbows. Hold each time to feel the pull along the sides. Then return to upright position, and stretch upward on tiptoes. Lower arms. Exhale, lower heels, and relax. Repeat twice.

SUN SALUTE

1. Stand erect, feet together, hands with palms together in front of chest. Relax and clear your mind (3—4).
2. Inhale, raising arms high and bending back from the waist (3—5).
3. Exhale, bending forward with straight knees, and touch the toes (3—6).
4. Inhale, extending right leg back while keeping left foot between hands on the ground. Raise head and arch back (3-7).
5. Hold breath, extending left leg behind alongside E other so that the body forms a straight line resting OH outstretched hands and toes (3—8).
6. Exhale, resting back on your heels, arms extended forward, head down (3—9).
7. Inhale, pushing forward, first forehead, then nose, chin and chest touching ground and then pushing up, bending back upper half of body (3—10A, B, C)
8. Exhale, raising hips with straight legs. Your heels are first up (3—11) and then lowered, pressed flat against the ground. Whole body forms a triangle.
9. Inhale, bringing right foot forward, toes on a line with hands. Raise head and arch back (3—12).
10. Exhale, with hands to toes and head down as in step 3 (3-13).

11. Inhale, raising arms high over head and bending backward as in step 2 (3—14).
12. Exhale, lower arms and relax (3—15).
  Repeat, moving the left leg first. Do from 2 to 12 times.

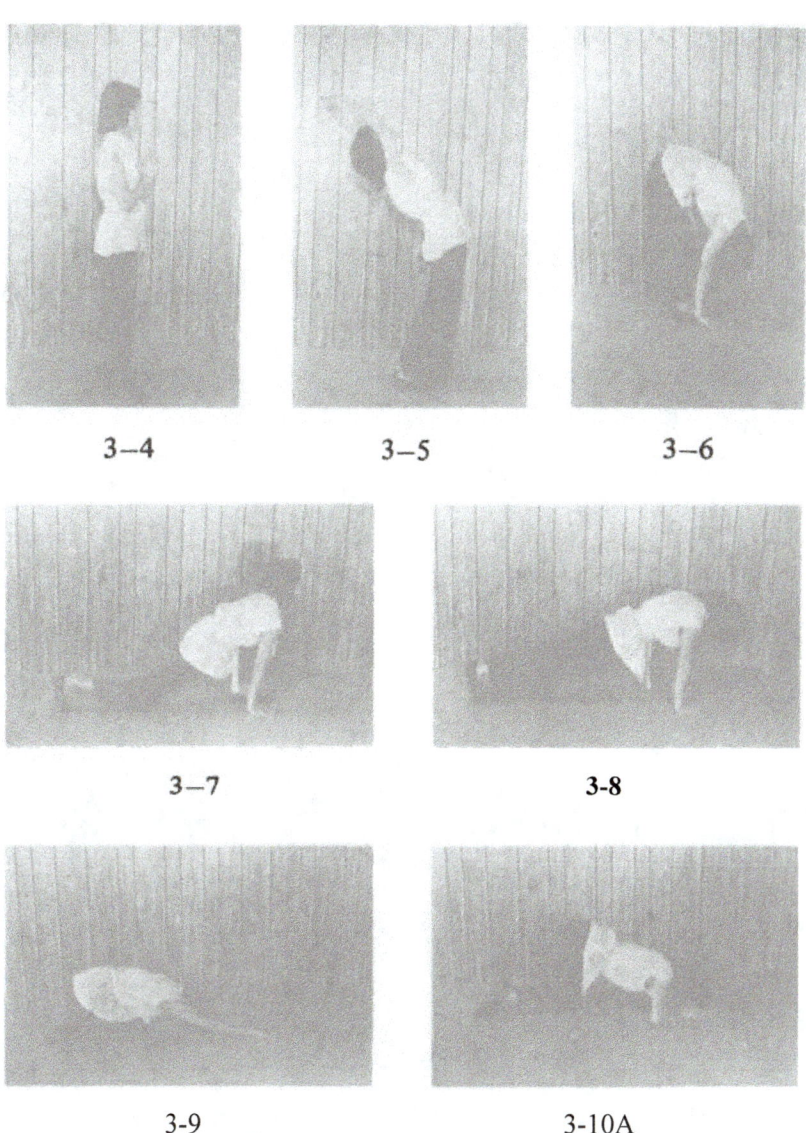

3–4   3–5   3–6

3–7   3-8

3-9   3-10A

THE FOUR COUNTING ALOUD EXERCISES

The voice is an expression of energy. Since you tend to concentrate on your count rather than the exercise, your body does not tense up and you relax farther into the position. Turning at the Waist

1. Feet are parallel and slightly more than shoulder width apart. Hips remain stationary throughout the exercise. Upper torso twists to the left side. Your left elbow bends and is drawn back to accentuate the twisting action (3—16). At the same time, the right arm and hand reach around the left shoulder. The head turns to the left as far as it will go. Count aloud: 1,2, 3, 4. With each count as you relax into the position, twist farther back.

2. In one flowing motion, reverse the procedure moving to the right side (3—17). Again count aloud to 4 and relax into the position. Each side will do this series 5 times for a total of 10.

Four to the Floor

Stand erect with feet parallel, together or shoulder width apart. Keep legs straight during this entire exercise. Bend at waist reaching down with both hands. Touch the floor as far as possible to the extreme left (3—18), counting aloud — 1. 2. Move your hands in a wide circle to the right, stopping at 45 degree intervals, counting aloud-2(3-19), 3(3-20).

Move to the extreme ri映t for a count of 4(3—21).

3-16

3-17

3-18

In a continuing action, bend as far backwards as possible, hands on the hips for support (3—22). Count aloud to 4. Move into the original upright position, and repeat the series, always moving to the left first. Repeat the series 10 times.

Right to Left Over Head

1. Stand erect with the feet parallel shoulder width or less apart. The body does not turn or lean forward during this exercise. In a single action, the left arm and hand reach down the left leg as far as possible drawing the body with it (3-23). At the same time the right hand reaches over the head as far as possible. The body stretches into the position as you count aloud - 1,2,3,4-

3-19   3-20   3-21

3-22   3-23   3-24

2. In a continuing flowing motion, the body will bend to the right repeating the action as in step 1 — Right arm moving down right leg, left arm over head (3—24), counting aloud — 1,2,3,4. Each side will do a total of 5.

Forehead to Knees

1. Stand erect with the feet together or a couple inches apart. Bend forward at the waist, keeping legs straight. Grab the calves with the hands and draw the forehead towards the knees (3—25) for an aloud count of 4. 2. Return to an upright position. Bend backwards at the waist, hands on hips (3—26), for an aloud count of 4. Repeat the complete exercise 10 times.

SINGLE ARM EXTENSION

1. Stand erect, feet together. Raise your right arm, level with shoulder, palm down. Inhale, reaching out as far as possible with your right fingers, moving only from the waist out (3—27). Hold position and breath for a few seconds.

2. Exhale, returning to original position. Do 3 times for the right arm. Repeat the above exercise using the left arm. Do 3 times.

3-25

3-26   3-27   3-28

MA BO-GUNG BO
1. Assume a Ma Bo (horse) stance. Both feet remain flat on the floor throughout this exercise. Extend the arms straight out to the sides. Moving slowly, inhale steadily while twisting the body to the left. Keep arms extended at shoulder height. As the body twists to the left, the right knee straightens with the left knee remaining bent, but twisted, creating a Gung Bo position (3—28). Hold this Gung Bo position for a slow count of 3.
2. Exhaling, return to beginning position. Repeat, moving to the right side. Do 3 times each side.

CAT STRETCH
1. Kneel on hands and knees so that your back is parallel to the floor, arm and legs perpendicular like legs of a table, palms forward (3—29). Inhale and slowly hump your back, sucking your stomach in and relaxing head and neck (3—30). Hold position and breath 5 to 10 seconds. Exhale and return to kneeling position.
2. Inhale and raise right leg, stretching it back and up (3—31). Keep head high, trying to touch bottom of foot

3-29

3-30

3-31

3-32

to head. Hold position and breath.

3. Exhaling, bring leg forward and try to press doubled- up knee to forehead (3—32). Do not touch the leg to the floor as you come forward. Do 3 to 5 times with the right leg and then switch to the left leg, repeating 3 to 5 times.

KNEE BEND

1. Stand firmly on left leg to steady your balance. Bend your right knee in front as high as possible. Clasp your leg below knee with both hands. Inhale. Pull knee in toward your chest (3—33). Breathe freely and stretch your spine upward for about 10 to 15 seconds. Concentrate on an object at eye level to steady your balance. 2. Exhale, lower your leg and relax. Stand on your right leg, bend left knee and repeat the same movements. Repeat 4 times each leg.

SINGLE LEG STAND

2. Stand firmly on your right leg, arms relaxed at your sides. Bend your right leg. Wrap your left foot around the calf of your right leg (3—34). Relax and hold the position at least 10 seconds.

3. Lower your left foot to the floor and without readjusting the pbsition of your left foot, bend your left knee and raise your right foot and wrap it around your

3—33

3-34

left calf. Hold the position at least 10 seconds. Repeat 3 times each leg.

BACK BEND

Lie on your back, feet flat on the floor and drawn up towards your buttocks. Curve arms back over your head, palms flat on floor, fingertips pointing towards your shoulders (3—35). Push your body up, keeping feet flat on the floor (3—36). Hold position 10 seconds and slowly lower your body to the floor.

JACKKNIFE

1. Lie on your back, arms extended on the floor over your shoulders. Jackknife your legs, torso and arms up, hands touching toes, balancing on a point slightly above the buttocks (3—37).
2. Return to the floor. Repeat 10 times.

KNEE PRESSES number 1

1. Lie flat on your back. Inhale and double up your left knee. Pull it back hard against your chest with both

3-35

3—36

3-37

3-38

hands. At the same time, raise your head and bring your chin over your left knee. Right leg straight, raise it 2 or 3 inches off the floor (3—38). Hold position and breath for a few seconds.

2. Slowly exhaling, without lowering legs or head to the floor, rotate the position — left leg extending a couple inches off the floor; right knee doubling up, both hands pulling the right knee back and chin coming over your right knee. Repeat 5 to 10 times each leg.

KNEE PRESSES number 2

Do the Knee Presses number 1 keeping both arms straight and extended at your sides about 2 or 3 inches from the floor (3-39). Try to extend your chin over your bent knee without the pressure of your hands. Repeat 5 to 10 times each leg.

FORWARD BEND number 1

1. In a sitting position, legs together and extended in front of body, raise your arms high over your head, stretching spine up.

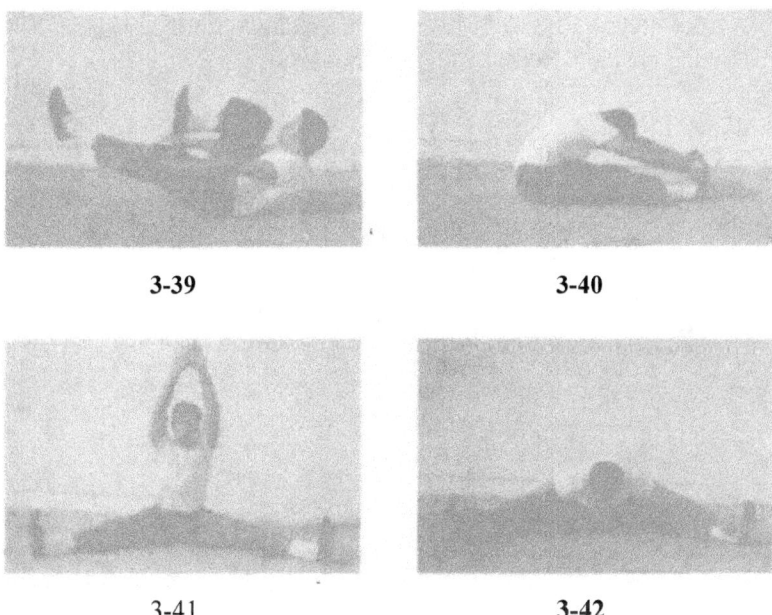

3-39   3-40

3-41   3-42

2. Exhale, lean forward and catch your toes (3-40). Keep your knees straight. Relax and hold the position for 20 seconds. Slowly return to a sitting position.

FORWARD BEND number 2
1. Spread legs wide apart, raise arms high over head, stretching spine up (3-41). Reach your right hand to your right foot and the left hand to left foot (3—42). Lean your body forward attempting to touch your face to the floor. Relax and hold for a 20 count. Slowly return to a sitting position.

FORWARD BEND number 3
Do as in the Forward Bend number 2, but keep your arms together. Reach first for the left foot (3—43). Hold. Release. Stretch up, and keeping arms together, reach for the right foot. Be sure to come out of the stretch slowly.

UPPER THIGH STRETCH
2. Sit, spine straight, your legs spread to form a 90 degree angle at the crotch. Bend your right leg, bringing the heel back against the hip, keeping your right knee on the floor.
3. Slowly lower yourself to a prone position, maintaining the 90 degree angle, keeping the right knee on the floor (3-44). Relax and hold for a 20 count. Return slowly to the original sitting position. Repeat with the other leg.

3T3

3-44

INNER THIGH STRETCH

1. Sit, spine straight. The bottom of your feet together, pull your heels in as close as possible to your crotch while keeping your knees down.

2. Gently push your knees down toward the floor with your elbows. Clasping your toes, bend forward and bring your forehead down toward the floor (3—45). Relax and hold the position for a 20 count.

STANDING SIDE SPLITS

Stand erect, your arms relaxed at your sides. Begin to move your feet out to the sides, keeping your upper body erect. Move out until you "feel" the stretch (3—46). Relax and hold the position. When you do not "feel it" any longer, move your feet out a little farther.

3-45   3-46

3—47   3-48   3-49

WOOD BLOCK STRETCH

Take 2 pieces of 2 by 4, each 12 inches long. Cut the high side of each board at a 30 degree angle, so that you can stand the boards on the 2 inch edge and place your feet at a 30 degree angle.

1. Place the boards 2 to 3 inches apart so that the 30 degree angle cuts are side by side, one angling up, the other angliiig down. Hrmly place your feet on the 30 degree angle cut of the boards, left heel raised, right lowered (3-47). Keep body erect. Raise your left arm, stretch upward with your left hand while at the same time stretching down with your right hand (3-48). Maintain this position for a slow count of 50. Reverse the wood angles and reverse the exercise.

2. A variation of number 1 — Keep the same feet position, but raise the right arm and stretch the left arm down for a slow count of 50.

These boards can be used in various ways. Put the boards at the same angles. Place your feet on the boards, heels down. Reach down trying to touch the flcxir (3-49). Experiment; find what position *stretches your* muscles.

QUESTIONS STRETCHING

1. What qualities are developed by stretching?
2. Name five basic needs that must be filled to maintain physical fitness.
3. What is the difference between stretching a muscle and developing a muscle?
4. Why should the body be flexible when doing technique?
5. Why should you not tug, strain or bounce strenuously when stretching a muscle?
6. What is meant by "feel it" when stretching?

CHAPTER 4
POWER EXERCISES
STATION TRAINING
TRAINING SCHEDULE
TECHNIQUE CALENDAR

The level of concentrated energy flow (Chapter 2) depends a great deal on physical energy potential.

This power potential can be greatly magnified in a short period of time by:

Power Exercise — specific exercises to stimulate and expand proper muscle groups

Station Training — organization of the exercises into a structured pattern for efficient training

Training Schedule — integration of the power exercises into your o^r-all training program

Technique Calendar — evaluation of each area of growth

POWER EXERCISES

The intensity of your applied technique depends a great deal on your mental-physical strength level and the coordination of mind-body to create a power base (Part 2). The following exercises will increase your strength and develop your mind-body coordination. Concentrate totally on each specie activity. Demand full participation of all the muscle groups needed to perfonn each task. The basic exercise offered here mainly develop the upper torso, expand energy intensity level for application of technique and increase endurance. If a specific breathing is not outlined, develop a deep, rhythmical pattern. Do not begin an exercise until you understand its purpose and application. After a strenuous workout, lie down and savasana (the relaxation pose described in the breathing exercises). Mentally allow the tightness and stiffness to dissolve.

CAUTION: If you have problems with any ligaments or joints, do not do the exercises which work with these ligaments or joints. If you experience acute pain at any time, stop and rest.

WRIST ROLL

Purpose

Used to develop hand grip, wrist, forearm, shoulder and upper back. Also used to train the arms to be independent of body strength and to develop endurance in the extended arms.

Equipment Needed

Two 5 pound weights attached to a handle by a rope or cord. The length of the cord should be such that when you are in the proper beginning position, the weight will barely be off the floor.

First Position

Stand vertical with the feet parallel and a little less than shoulder width apart. Hold the handle at each end so that you have a firm grip and there is enough room in the center of the handle to wind up all the cord without interfering with your hand movement. The weight should be 2 to 3 inches from the floor (4-1 and 2).

Raise your arms in front of you with the elbows locked and the palms facing down. Your hands through this whole exercise stay in the area between your ears and your shoulders, no higher or lower. *Do not bend the elbows* af *any time.*

Position the cord so that it is on the inside of the handle (closest to you). Without moving your arms, steadily wind up the cord on the handle (4—3), using only wrist action. *Both hands* must equally raise the

4-1

4-2

weight. Roll up the cord until the weight touches your hands (4—4). Then lower it until it is 2 or 3 inches from the floor. This exercise should be done initially for at least one minute each time. You should not stop moving the weight during this minute. When you can roll it up and down twice in one minute, you are ready for the second exercise.

Second Position

Position the cord so that it is on the outside of the handle (farthest from you). Do the basic exercise as in the first position, only now you lift the weight by rolling the cord up on the outside (4-5) for one minute. When you can roll it up and down once in one minute you are ready for the third position.

Third Position

Stand against a wall so that your head, buttocks and heels are flat

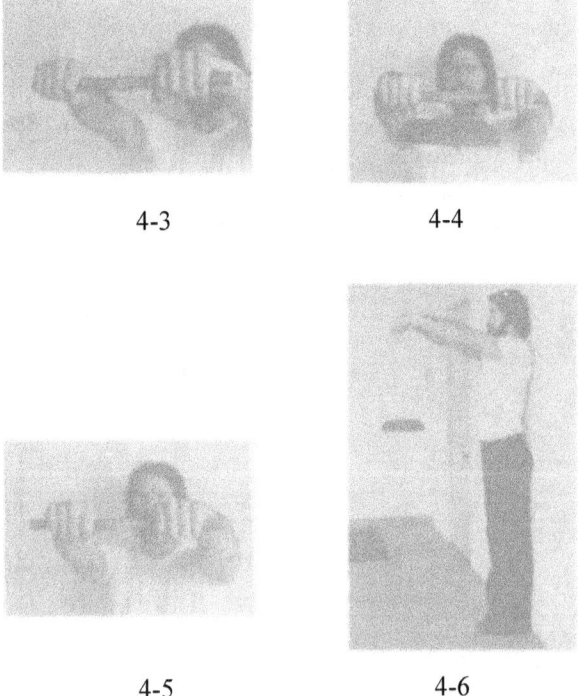

4-3   4-4

4-5   4-6

against it (4—6). Without moving these parts of the body off the wall, do the wrist roll as described in the first position (cord on the inside) for two minutes. When you can do three up and down actions of the weight, you are ready to do position 4.

Fourth Position

This is done the same as position 3 only raise the weight with the cord on the outside of the handle. Do it for no less than 1½ minutes.

Comments

The wrist roll is a very strenuous exercise and should not be rushed. Give your muscles a chance to develop naturally before moving to the next position. You should feel ready to change rather than just be tired of doing the first position.

This exercise will be part of an over-all exercise pattern (Station Training) which will be presented in this chapter. If you cannot buy a wrist roll set-up, use a 1% inch wooden dowel, 16 inches long. Drill a hole through the center. Thread a length of nylon cord through the hole and secure it with a knot. At the other end of the cord, tie an object which weighs 5 or 10 pounds. (A plastic Clorox container filled with water is good; its handle makes it ' asy to secure to the cord.)

CAUTION: Use common sense when determining how much weight to use initially (5 or 10 pounds). Do not strain yourself.

TIGER PUSH-UPS
Purpose

To develop the elbow, biceps, triceps, shoulder and back muscles.

Exercise

Kneel on the floor with your heels against the wall. Keep your back parallel to the floor and your hands turned inward so the fingertips touch and are directly below your mouth (4—7). Raise your body until your arms and legs are straight, with the elbows and Gees locked (4—8). Without bending your knees, allow your elbows to bend outward, dropping your body down until your forehead lightly touches your hands (4—9). Return to your raised position. Do this exercise for one minute without resting. When you can do 10 tigers in one minute, increase your time 30 seconds and work up to 15 tigers in the 1½ minutes. Then add 30 seconds more and do the tigers for a solid 2 minutes.

Comments

At first most people experience difficulty with this exercise. Be patient; take your time. It is wise to push yourself a little, but unwise if you strain yourself and thus limit future training. If you have any shoulder problems, avoid this exercise.

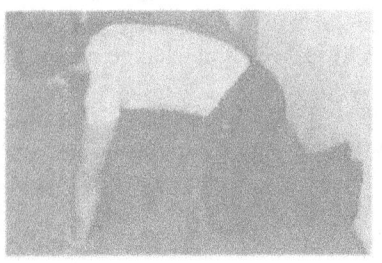
4-7

4-8

4-9

HAND GRIPS
Purpose

To develop grip and forearms.

Equipment Needed

A pair of athletic hand grips and a watch or clock with a second sweep hand.

Exercise

Stand upright in a relaxed position with the feet about 4 inches apart and a hand grip in each hand with the handles toward the floor (4-10). As fast as you can, close (4—11) and open the grips completely for 15 seconds. At the end of the first 15 seconds hold the grips closed for 15 seconds, squeezing them as hard as you can. At the end of the second 15 *seconds, open and close them rapidly for another 15 seconds and then for the last 15 seconds hold them tight again. This exercise lasts for one minute. When you feel you can do it longer, add 15 seconds. Do not strain yourself. You can add 15 second segments until a full two minutes has been reached.

Comments

Get a strong pair of hand grips (steel) rather than the plastic ones you find in most sporting stores. Always alternate the squeeze grip with the open-close pattern. If you cannot get any hand grips, buy two inexpensive firm rubber balls at a toy store.

4-10   4-11

STRETCH SPRING
Purpose

To develop the wrist and a forward flow of energy through the arm.

Equipment Needed

Athletic stretch springs or surgical rubber that you can secure at one end and attach a handle to the other. Surgical rubber can usually be purchased in a drug store or fishing supply store. Be sure it is heavy duty.

Exercise

 Attach one end of the surgical rubber or stretch spring to a solid base. Grasp the handle attached to the other end and extend the rubber or spring out until a strong reversing pressure is felt (4—12). Keep this constant straining pressure at all times. Without moving the arm, raise the closed hand in an upward arc (4—13) and then angle it downward as far as it will go (4-14). Keep up this arcing action for one minute. Then switch arms and do it with the other one for one minute. Switch back and repeat with the original and then again to the second arm so a total of two minutes per arm is achieved.

Comments

Do not lean into the pressure. Stay upright and let the arm support the strain.

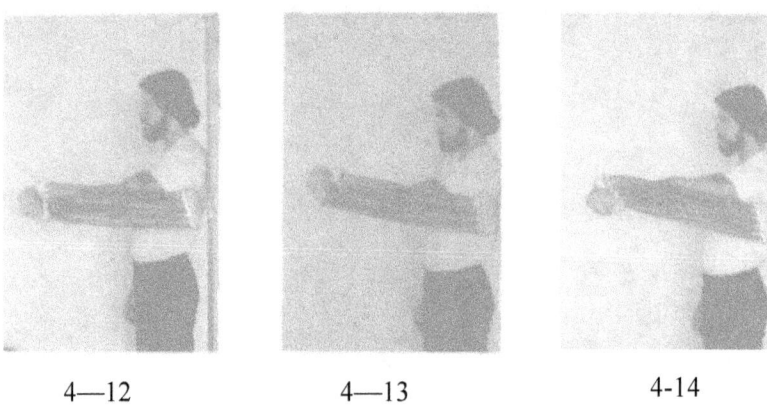

4—12   4—13   4-14

DOUBLE DOAN CHI
Purpose

To develop the upper torso and create an intense forward flow. It also helps with shoulder flexibility so the elbows will move towards your centerline easier.

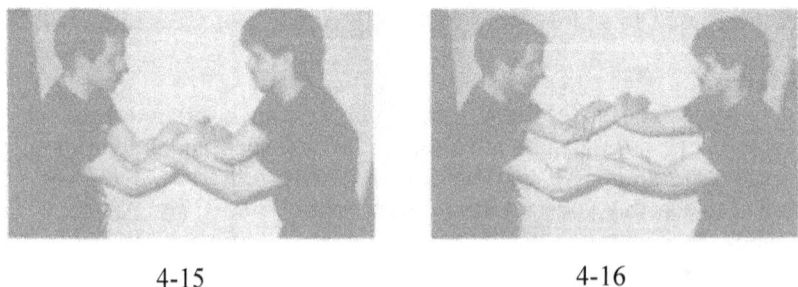

4-15   4-16

Equipment Needed

Either a partner or a 2 inch rubber inner tube strip.

With a Partner

Place your arms together at the elbows and extend the forearms parallel to the floor, palms up. Your partner will place his hands on the outside of your wrists (4—15). As your partner applies a steady pressure toward you and inward, you begin to move your arms forward and outward against your partner's pressure. Your partner applies sufficient pressure to make it hard for you to move outward, yet not so much pressure that you will be stopped from moving. Extend your aims forward as far as they will go and outward to the edge of your partner's body (4—16). Exhale slowly as you extend. Once your arms are extended fully your partner begins to push your hands towards one another and back. You resist as much as you can while letting your arms slowly return to their original position. Inhale slowly as you return. *Do not rest* once the arms are back in the starting position. Immediately begin again. Do this for one minute. Then switch with your partner and let him do it for one minute. You will do it once more and switch again with your partner so that each of you does it for a full two minutes.

With Inner Tube

The basic action is the same as that done with a partner. You extend, exhaling and slowly return to the

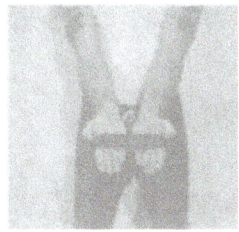
4-17

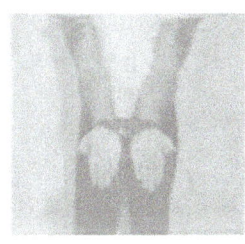
4—18

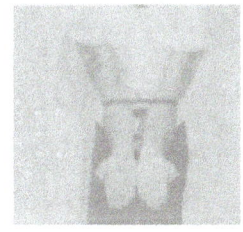
4—19

original position, inhaling. Do this for one minute with the inner tube around both your palms (4—17). Rest one minute. Do it with the inner tube around both wrists (4-18) for one minute. Rest one minute. Do it with the tube around both elbows (4—19) for one minute.

Comments

Keep the pressure constant without relaxing at any time.

SLOW PUNCHING WITH WRIST ROLL
Purpose

To develop shoulder, upper back and extension muscles in arm.

Equipment Needed

One 5 pound wrist roll and one 5 pound weight which can be added to the 5 pound wrist roll. Initially do this exercise with only 5 pounds; work up to the 10 pounds.

Exercise

First: Before starting, roll the cord up so the weight is a couple inches below your right hand. Place your right arm in a cocked ready position, elbow close to your body. Hold the handle and cord in your grip so that the weight will not slip. Keep your fist vertical (4-20). Stand relaxed with the right foot leading slightly. Slowly extend your arm parallel to the floor so when it is fully extended the hand will be at the center of your body (4—21). As you extend, slowly exhale. By the time

4-20　　　　　　　　4-21　　　　　　　　4-22

you reach the centerline, all the air in your lungs should be expelled. Inhale slowly as you withdraw your arm back into the starting position. Do this for one minute. Rest for one minute by setting the weight down and moving your arm in a gentle circular motion (4-22).

Second': Unwind the cord so that the weight is half way between your shoulders and the floor. Repeat the first exercise. Rest. Rotate arm.

Third: Unwind the cord so that the weight is 2 to 3 inches from the floor. Repeat exercise 1. Rest. Rotate arm.

Switch arms and repeat the 3 positions on the other arm.
Comments
Watch your breathing. Do not hurry the motion.

HEAVY BAG
Purpose
To develop endurance and constant flow of forward energy.
Equipment Needed
Heavy bag, gloves to use when working with the bag and a timer.
Exercise

Stand in a relaxed position in front of the bag. Free yourself of any mental distractions. Once you begin, the exercise will be one long continuous flow of energy. Breathe in such a manner so that you can exhale in short

4-23

4—24

4-25

bursts everytime you hit the bag.

Step in towards the bag and hit it with a strong straight blow similar to a boxer's strike (4-23). Once you hit the bag and move it back, you should try to keep hitting it so that the bag stays away from you without moving back to its original position until you stop (4—24). Do this for 1 minute.

SKIPPING ROPE
Purpose
To develop rhythm, endurance and the ability to move on the balls of the feet.
Equipment Needed
Skipping rope.
First Exercise
Skip in a right-left pattern similar to a boxer. Never allow your feet to move more than 2 inches off the floor. Stay on the balls of the feet at all times (4-25). Do this in a steady motion for 2 minutes. Pick up speed only as your endurance increases.
Second Exercise
Skip with both feet leaving the floor at the same time. Count aloud each time your feet leave the floor. Start with a count of 50 and work up to 250.

GENERAL SUGGESTIONS
We could go on and on listing exercises, but the few here should give you a base to begin your program. These exercises may be a part of your initial training program. Add selected exercises as your proficiency and strength expands.

Working out for physical well being is a life time project which involves not only physiological training but good nutritional and personal habits. It is up to each individual to determine the level to which he wishes to develop, then create a program to accomplish his goals.

STATION TRAINING

This section is to be used only after you have learned the over-all basic principles and exercises of this volume.

Station training is simply the structuring out of an exercise pattern which allows you to cover a variety of techniques and general exercises in a short period of time.

You should schedule only as many exercises as you will do in one day. It is best to establish a program that takes only 15 minutes or less. This allows you to do the stations twice a day — once early in your over-all training schedule and once again towards the end. Do these station exercises for at least one week before altering them. You will want to alter them to correspond with the techniques you are working on at that time. Two basic programs are listed here. You can follow these or establish your own.

General Instructions

Follow the order of these stations. You may start at different stations but keep them in the same order. For instance, start on the 4th, go to the 5th, 6th, 1st, 2nd and 3rd. Always put a soft exercise after a hard one or you will "burn out" too quickly. Allow one full minute for each station and only 10 seconds between stations. Once you begin, totally concentrate on the station you are doing. "Burn" for one minute with full intensity. Be sure to allow only a maximum of 10 seconds to pass before beginning the next station.

FIRST STATIONS

Equipment Needed

Wrist roll, hand grips and a timer.

First Station*. 10 pound wrist roll (away from wall, inside twist)
Second Station: Right and left Sole Kick Exercise
Third Station: Duck Walk (Chapter 6, Single Unit Moving Exercise 2)
Fourth Station*. Hand Grips (15 second sequence, rapid) *Fifth Station:* Double Chung Choie Rapid Punching (stationary)
Sixth Station: Tiger Push-ups

SECOND STATIONS

Equipment Needed

2 inch inner tube strip, jumping rope, heavy bag, TV and 耳 timer.
First Station: 10 pound wrist roll (against wall, outside twist)
Second Station: Skip a step closing
Third Station: Heavy bag striking

Fourth Station: TV reflex punching
Fifth Station:, Jumping rope
Sixth Station: Shuffle step with spring step on the % step *Seventh Station:* Double Doan Chi (inner tube on wrist) *Eighth Station:* Double Chung Choie closing (straight)

If you have a partner, you may add partner exercises such as shadow closing (straight and evasive), high Taun Sao-low Goang Sao exercise or double Chung Choie closing against a pad. If two of you are doing a station requiring two people, you will do the exercise for one minute; then switch and let your partner do the exercise. This doubles the length of time for the stations.

If two of you work together on a station requiring each person to work individually, you will have to have two sets of hand grips, wrist rolls or whatever equipment is needed. If you do not have two sets of equipment, you can do one of the individual stations; your partner can do a different individual station, and you can work together in the stations that require partners.

Station training helps you organize a lot of important exercise into a compact period of time. This allows you more time to spend on hand techniques, dummy practice or anything else you may wish to do.

Each station lasts a short time, but if you concentrate fully on getting as much as you can out of that one minute, you will be surprised at how well and rapidly you develop.

TRAINING SCHEDULE

TIME SCHEDULE

The time you spend on your weekly program and the number of techniques you practice depend on three things:

1. Time available to train

How much time, on a daily basis, can you consistently set aside for training? Since you are adding techniques from previous chapters to each new program, you will either have to add more time to your daily practice as you start each new chapter, or you will have to lengthen the total time spent on each chapter's program. It might be helpful to establish goals for developing proficiency in a technique within a certain amount of time. This can help you determine how much time you should spend each day. Although the graph allows for working out seven days a week, it is recommended that y use Sunday for reflection and introspection.

2. Amount and type of technique

Some principles and applied techniques are short and simple. Others are more difficult and require more time. Rereading the chapter a few times before you begin will develop a feeling for identifying and separating the simple techniques from those that are complicated. Do not try to learn more than one complicated technique at a time; this will only add to the confusion.

3. Your rate of learning

Only practice will allow you to determine how quickly you can understand and apply technique. *Do not be in a hurry.* Give your mind and body a chance to develop a natural understanding of the concepts and applications. As you move from chapter to chapter you will develop an inner awareness of your basic learning potential and you can speed up or slow down accordingly.

SAMPLE COMPLETE TRAINING SCHEDULE

An example of a full training schedule is included here (Training Schedule A, Graph 3—A) to give you an overview of how the schedule will look when you reach the end of this book. Although you will not understand it yet, as you go through the book note that the schedule is following a certain order. You may change the general order for practicing techniques, but it is recommended that you maintain the breathing, meditation and stretching order as they will complement your daily workout. The basic outline offered here is:

Breathing: To stimulate the mind and body relation ship

Meditation: To eliminate disturbances and distractions

Stretching: To prepare the body for moving as natural ly as possible

First Series of Station Training: For intensity

Stances and
Basic Body
Motion: To organize the various body segments into a single unit

Training Schedule A, Graph 3—A

	technique	mon	tue	wed	thu	fri	sat	sun
	BREATHING	2	2	2	2	2	2	
	MEDITATION	2	2	2	2	2	2	
	STRETCHING	5	5	5	5	5	5	
STATION TRAINING	WRIST ROLL IV	2	2	2	2	2	2	
	T.V. PUNCHING	2	2	2	2	2	2	
	HEAVY BAG	2	2	2	2	2	2	
	SHADOW CLOSING	2	2	2	2	2	2	
	DOUBLE DOAN CHI	2	2	2	2	2	2	
STANCES	MISC. STANCES	15	15	15	15	15	15	
	MISC. HANDS	15	15	15	15	15	15	
	MISC. STRETCHING	10	10	10	10	10	10	
	MISC. STRIKES	10	10	10	10	10	10	
	MISC. KICKS	10	10	10	10	10	10	
2ND STATIONS	JUMP ROPE II	2	2	2	2	2	2	
	WRIST ROLL PUNCHING	2	2	2	2	2	2	
	DOUBLE CHUNG CHOIE CLOSE	2	2	2	2	2	2	
	HAND GRIPS	2	2	2	2	2	2	
	TIGERS	2	2	2	2	2	2	
ANGULAR CLOSING	MISC. CLOSING	15	15	15	15	15	15	

Hand
Techniques: To develop natural offensive and defensive actions in a primary perimeter

Striking
Techniques: To complement hand techniques

Kicking
Techniques: For long range control

Second Series of Station
Training: For intensity

Closing
Exercises: A bringing together of all body techniques into one flowing series of exercises.

BLANK TRAINING SCHEDULES

There is a blank training schedule at the end of the book for your convenience. You may make as many copies of it as you need. There is also a blank schedule at the end of this chapter. Begin to use this blank training schedule when you have finished reading this chapter. A sample training schedule has been worked out as a guide line (Training Schedule B, Graph 3—B).

The graph is divided into seven segments horizontally. In each segment on the extreme left hand side, you may insert the various techniques and exercises you plan to practice each week. As previously suggested you may use the top segment for breathing, meditation and stretching. In the remaining segments, insert the specific techniques and exercises that you plan to use. Note that the graph shows "Power Exercises**" in the second section. It is sub-divided into the various aspects of "Power Exercises", namely: Wrist Roll 1, Tigers and so forth.

The page is divided into several vertical segments: the days of the week and a blank in which a check mark can be inserted. Under the days of the week, insert the amount of time you plan to spend each day, in minutes, practicing and perfecting the techniques listed on the left side of the page. When you have spent the allotted time practicing any given technique area, place a check in the space provided for that

Training Schedule B, Graph 3—B

	technique	mon ✓	tue ✓	wed ✓	thu ✓	fri ✓	sat ✓	sun
	BREATHING	2	2	2	2	2	2	
	MEDITATION	2	2	2	2	2	2	
	STRETCHING	5	5	5	5	5	5	
1ST POWER EXERCISES	WRIST ROLL I	1	1	1	1	1	1	
	STRETCH SPRING	1	1	1	1	1	1	
	HAND GRIPS	1	1	1	1	1	1	
	TIGERS	1	1	1	1	1	1	
	STRETCHING	10	10	10	10	10	10	
2ND POWER EXERCISES	DOUBLE DOAN CHI	1	1	1	1	1	1	
	SKIPPING ROPE I	1	1	1	1	1	1	
	HEAVY BAG	1	1	1	1	1	1	
	WRIST ROLL PUNCHING	1	1	1	1	1	1	

technique on that day. If you have not practiced, leave the check area blank.

Using this blank graph to list your techniques and time schedule will hopefully help you become, not only more organized but more consistent in your training efforts. Be realistic when you fill out the weekly training schedule. Put down only what you wj " do rather than what you would like to do.

SAMPLE TRAINING SCHEDULES

When you begin a new chapter, make a notation on your new weekly training schedule indicating the techniques you have learned but that you feel need a little more practice. For instance, if you have already practiced hand exercises in a previous chapter but are not confident of all of them, put down "Mise Hands" on your graph. You then will allot time for working on the hand techniques that you feel need more training.

Your training schedule should allow only a short period of time on new techniques. At this point it is necessary to become familiar only with the basic purpose and application of each technique. Once you have become familiar with all the techniques in Volume 1, you can establish a more concentrated and lengthy practice period for each technique. You may find it is sometimes advantageous to practice only one technique for the whole week. Your judgment in settingup a weekly training schedule will improve as time goes on.

TECHNIQUE CALENDAR

To identify any increase in your proficiency as a martial artist, it will be necessary to establish a reference point which indicates your beginning or present ability. This reference point will include your overall present mind-body level in such areas as flexibility, power, speed and applied techniques. It gives you an opportunity to evaluate where you are now, in comparison to where you were a week ago, month ago, etc..

The way this reference point is determined is by using a Technique Calendar.

When filling out this calendar, you can list basic growth techniques such as meditation, stretching and power exercises as well as basic theory and applied technique.

To give a clear example of the scoring system used, a sample calendar is presented. Although the growth techniques will actually be listed first we will confine the example used to hand techniques.

SAMPLE TECHNIQUE CALENDAR

A technique calendar is a method of determining your rate of growth in specific areas. It is a way to list the techniques you study in the order that you learn them.

Note the sample calendar (Technique Calendar, Graph 4). Each technique is listed. The date the technique is first learned is entered in the first column. The year is entered at the top of the sheet. As you begin a new technique, add it to your list with the month and day in the proper space. You will use an evaluation system using numbers one through ten. One denotes the beginning of a technique and ten denotes the mastery of the technique.

An example of a listing from your technique calendar may be:

Taun Sao 4-1 [1] 5-5 [3] 6-30 [6]

In this example, April 1st was the starting date for learning Taun Sao. A beginning score of 1 was entered in the column headed by an [S] (score). On May 5, after studying the principle and application theory carefully, the grade was raised to 3. By June 30th, reasonable proficiency had been achieved in application and control so a score of 6 was given.

Be sure to list the techniques in the order learned. Keep in mind the higher the score the better you should be at understanding and applying the technique.

This numerical gauge is for personal use only and will have no relationship to anyone else's progress. If after an honest amount of effort you find your score still low (under 5) you should consult with your instructor and try to identify the difficulty.

This Technique Calendar gauge is also to let you judge overall growth for a specific period of time (6 months). With the advantages of reviewing your list and separating the weak and strong areas more time can be directed towards the techniques which need more attention.

Technique Calendar
Graph 1

Technique	Date	[S]	Date	[S]	Date	[S]
TAUN SAO	4-1	1	5-5	3	6-30	6
FOOK SAO	4-1	1	5-5	3	6-30	6
GOANG SAO	4-1	1	5-7	3	6-29	5
DIE JEONG	4-3	1	5-3	4	6-29	6
PAK SAO	4-3	1	5-3	3	7-1	5
LOP SAO	4-4	1	5-10		7-1	7
BONG SAO	4-4	1	5-10		7-4	5
HUENG SAO	4-4	1	5-15		7-4	6
BIL JEE	4-5	1	5-15		7-5	6

TRAINING SCHEDULE

technique	mon	tue	wed	thu	fri	sat	sun

QUESTIONS - POWER EXERCISES AND STATION TRAINING

1. Your intensity level for applying technique is dependent on two things. Name them.
2. What is a primary reason for TWCD power exercises?
3. What should you do when you experience acute pain while exercising?
4. Describe the proper way to do the 4 wrist roll exercises.
5. What does the tiger push-up develop?
6. What does the stretch spring exercise do?
7. Name three things that are developed by doing double Doan Chi.
8. How does the slow punching with wrist roll help you?
9. What is the primary reason for the heavy bag workout?
10. Name two exercises for skipping rope.
11. Name three things that are essential to develop physical well-being.
12. What is the purpose of station training?
13. Why schedule a soft exercise after a hard one?

QUESTIONS - TRAINING SCHEDULE AND TECHNIQUE CALENDAR

14. What factors must be considered when you determine your weekly training program?
15. Why is it helpful to set training goals?
16. What happens when you try and work on more than one complicated technique at once?
17. How can practice help you develop a better program?
18. Explain the importance of a training schedule.
19. How is a technique calendar used?
20. What should be done when you encounter a consistent difficulty with a technique?

CHAPTER 5
NINE CRITICAL PERIMETERS

Minimizing physical moves or efforts is a key to speed and/or efficient motion. Establishing a set area in which your body actions take place will limit flourishing and over-reacting and allow you to channel your techniques with a minimum of effort and the maximum of results.

Before evolving into hand, leg and body techniques, a defined area of exercise will be established so that the student can quickly distinguish between motion that is necessary and actions that are wasted.

In this chapter, the nine perimeters are individually described so the student will have a better overview of these positions. The application and use of the perimeters will be covered in later chapters. Here only the defined area of each perimeter is given along with general comments.

1. UPPER
PERIMETER Defined

This perimeter includes the head, neck, shoulders and torso down to the elbows (with the arms hanging by the side).

General Comments

Look at picture 5—1. You will notice the perimeter line angles from the eyes to the shoulders. This angling line eliminates corners, which are referred to as a dead space. This upper perimeter is a primary perimeter since most of the hand technique, both offensive and defensive, take place in this area. It is the hardest to protect since the majority of techniques are designed to penetrate this area and wasted motion can easily leave an open gate (exposed area). This perimeter is also an important source for converging your energy forward into the opponent (Converging Energy, Part 2).

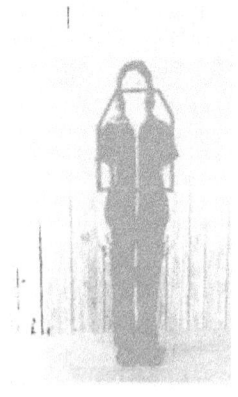

5-1

2. LOWER PERIMETER
Defined Area
The lower perimeter is that area between the hanging elbows and the groin (5—2).
General Comments
The line angling from the elbow to the hip is to eliminate dead space. The lower perimeter contains both the center of balance and the pivoting axis for generating explosive power. It is very difficult for an opponent to reach this area (referred to as a limited access area) without opening his own perimeters.

3. LOWER GATE
Defined Area
The lower gate is that area from the groin down (5—3). **General Comments**
This is the primary base for power, balance and mobility. Control of this gate will insure maximum efficiency of the upper perimeters. Since the success of all offensive and defensive technique is dependent on a stable, yet flexible base, the importance of the lower gate cannot be over-emphasized.

4. INNER PERIMETER
Defined Area
Place your elbow in the elbow pocket and extend your forearm forward parallel to the floor with the hand open, palm toward your body. The inner perimeter is that area between your chest and the front line at the open palm area.

5-2

5-3

5y

Elbow Pocket

The elbow can be placed in its pocket by hanging the arm straight down by the side and lifting the forearm parallel to the floor (5-4). The circled area in the picture is the elbow pocket. At no time should the elbow move farther back than its pocket position.

General Comments

The front line of this perimeter is the closest you will allow your opponent to come to you. This tight position limits you to slipping palm strikes, short backfists and a variety of elbow smashes. The effectiveness of the arms, both offensively and defensively, is greatly reduced if the elbows move back of their pockets.

5. OUTER PERIMETER
Defined Area

Place your right hand in a vertical position at the center of your chest, slightly above the solar plexis (5—5). (This imaginary line extending outward from the center of your chest is referred to as your centerline.) Extend the hand straight out away from the body, keeping the hand vertical and facing the centerline (5-6). When you can no longer extend it and keep it vertical with the palm still facing centerline, stop. Keep the arm in place, turn the palm toward the body, parallel to the floor (5—7). The outer perimeter is that area between the front line of the inner perimeter and the front line formed by the extended open palm.

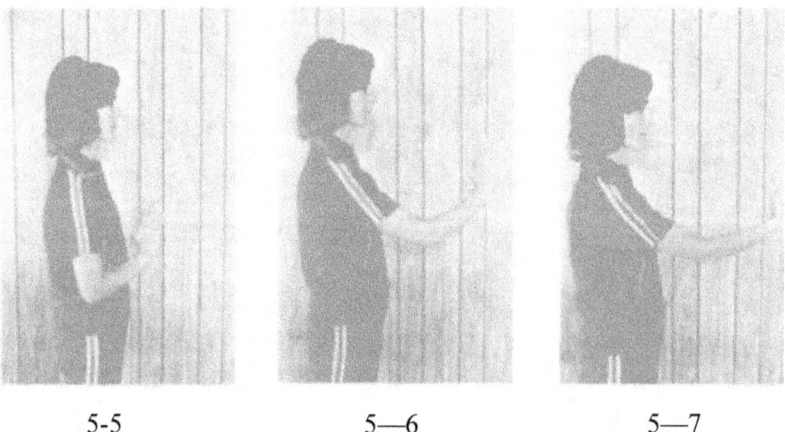

5-5   5—6   5—7

General Comments

This extended point is the farthest you will allow your opponent to move away from you while in a fighting situation. The major techniques can be done in this area from the inner perimeter to the extended palm. In this area, you can also utilize fully your speed, power, flexibility and trapping principles.

6. EXTENDED PERIMETER
Defined Area

Stand erect. Extend a leg forward parallel to the floor. Point the toes straight out (5—8). The extended perimeter is that area from the edge of the outer perimeter to the tip of the extended toes.

General Comments

Once the hands exceed the outer perimeter, they lose much of their power and control because the arms are almost fully extended and have little, if any, powerload from the elbow. The only effective weapons in the extended perimeter are the legs.

7. RIGHT PERIMETER
Defined Area

Split the body down the front center on your centerline. All that area on the right side is the right perimeter (5-9). **General Comments**

The right arm and leg will function 98% of the time in this

5—8

5-9

5-10

area. Extending the right hand over the centerline to the left side shifts the energy to the opposite side and exposes a wide area in the right upper perimeter.

8. LEFT PERIMETER
Defined Area
Split the body down the front center on your centerline. All that area on the left side is the left perimeter (5-10).
General Comments
98% of action here will be done by the left hand and leg.

9. KILL RANGE
Defined Area
The kill range is your opponenfs outstretched leg length (toes pointed straight ahead) plus three inches (5—11). The line at that point of the opponenfs extended leg length plus three inches is referred to as the edge of the kill range. **Exercise**
Stand loose and relaxed. Choose a partner who is either taller or shorter than you. He will move in a half circle in front and to the sides of you, coming in close to you and moving farther back. When you feel he is on or barely out of your kill range, tell him to stop. Check your judgement by having your partner raise and extend his leg toward you to see if he is in or out of the kill range. Sinee a lot of closing technique depends on precise distance (Part 2, Angular Closing Techniques), it is important that you instinctively are able to judge the opponenfs distance.

General Comments
This is one of the most critical perimeters to learn. It is this space that will allow you to evaluate, move and feel out your opponent. When your opponent is on or outside this line, he, because of the need to stretch or make two actions to reach you, cannot move without telegraphing. If you do not either withdraw or attack when your opponent enters the kill range, then your opponent has an excellent opportunity to strike without you having time to react. If you stand too far away from your opponent

5-11

(a distance greater than the determined kill range), you will limit your own ability to reach your opponent (close the gap).

EXERCISES TO PRACTICE THESE NINE PERIMETERS WILL BE COVERED IN LATER CHAPTERS IN CONJUNCTION WITH TECHNIQUE.

BLENDING OF PERIMETERS

The lines of your upper and lower perimeters angle, blending with the opponenfs upper and lower perimeters (5—12). If there is a great difference in size between you and your opponent, that difference can be equalized by blending your perimeter (5—13). If the opponent is much broader or taller than you, then his arms can hook quite effectively around your perimeter (5—14). If he is shorter or thinner, he will be able to use strong technique inside your perimeter. By aligning your perimeter to his you equalize any body difference so your basic offensive and defensive techniques will still apply (5-15).

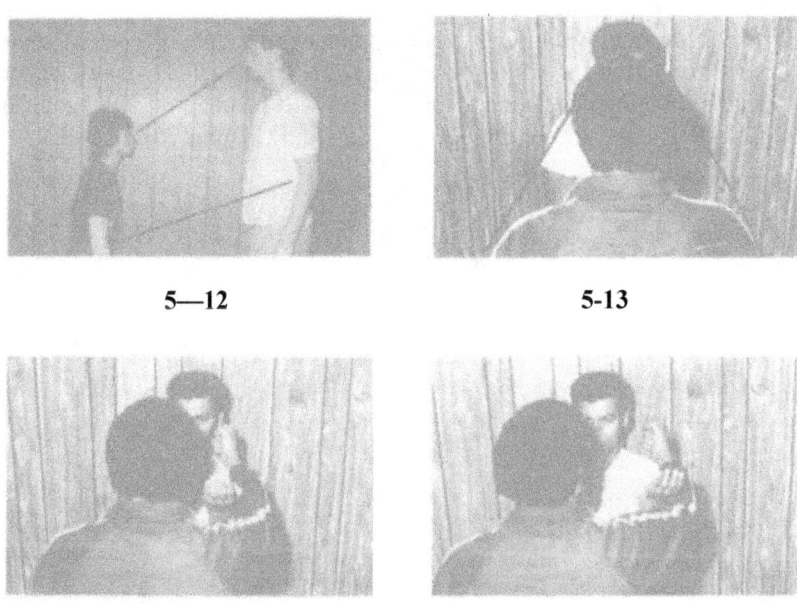

5—12

5-13

5-14

5-15

JOAN SOM - CENTERLINE PRINCIPLE

This principle allows each hand to act independently of the other while keeping the body in such a position that you can *touch your opponent with either hand at any time* (5-16). **General Comments**

This is a simple principle but one of the most important ones of this system. The efficiency of trapping and sticking hands as well as of the Lin Sil Die Dar (Total Attack Theories) relies to a great extent on this one principle. To break the centerline (5—17) weakens the versatility of this theory.

Using both hands independently of one another, yet having them work together as a team, allows for a much wider range of effective inside techniques, since both hands can function offensively, defensively or both. Maintaining your centerline (keeping square to the opponent) gives you the opportunity to perform double hand techniques; this greatly restricts the opponent^ offensive potential. Keeping the centerline constant also allows you maximum use of your energy since it is flowing directly toward your opponent. **Floating Centerline**

When striking and trapping your opponent, you may bend the centeriine to the right or left as much as, but no more than, fifteen degrees. Ulis allows you to pivot your energy and express it in a more explosive manner. (To be covered in Part 2, Power Base and Speed).
Pivoting Centeriine

Sometimes, because of your opponent's motion, you must pivot your body in order to keep your centerline constant. This is referred to as the pivoting centerline. (Application will be covered in Chapter 6, Left, Right and Reverse Qosed Bi Jong and Chapter 7, Lop Sao.)

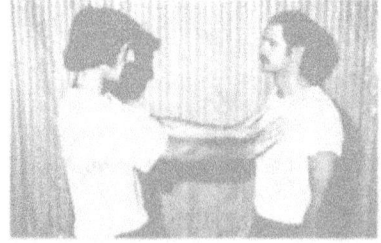
5-16

5-17

Pivoting Exercise

To the Left: Stand upright in a relaxed position. Feet are a little less than shoulder width apart. The right foot is slightly ahead of the left foot. Knees are slightly bent and springy. In a flowing motion, shift your whole body and feet position 90 degrees to the left. This may be done in one of two ways: either by moving your weight to the balls of your feet and skimming the heels to the new position or by pivoting with the weight on the heels and skimming the balls of your feet to the new position. In either case your balance must shift at the same time. Practice this movement to the left until you have developed a smooth relaxed shift of position.

To the Right: You can use the same basic motion as the left pivot as long as your left foot is leading and you do not pivot beyond 45 degrees.

To pivot beyond 45 degrees to the right when your right foot is leading, you will have to step slightly forward with the left foot; shift your weight to the balls of your feet, and skimming your heels over the floor, pivot to your new position.

In the actual application of the pivot action a lot will depend on the amount of motion by your opponent. Your motion can range from a full pivot step to a simple rotating off your knees rather than a shifting of the feet.

QUESTIONS - NINE CRITICAL PERIMETERS

Answer the questions below as clearly and in as much detail as you can. Etch the perimeters in your mind so that as you add leg and body techniques you will recognize when you break out of any perimeter.

1. List 2 reasons for establishing perimeters.
2. Name 2 aspects of the upper perimeter that make it important.
3. Name 2 important aspects of the lower perimeter.
4. Why do the perimeters angle down from the eyes to the shoulders and from the hanging elbows to the hips?
5. Why is the lower gate an important perimeter?
6. What is a disadvantage of using hand technique in the extended perimeter?
7. How do you gauge the kill range?
8. What is meant by the blending of perimeters?
9. Draw front and side views of an individual and draw in and label the 9 perimeters.

CHAPTER 6
STANCES

A stance can create a stable base from which spontaneity, speed, power and flexibility flow in a natural, unrestricted way; or it can create a prison in which you must conform to any number of restricted and mechanical motions.

BALANCE AND WEIGHT DISTRIBUTION

The center of balance control in the body is generally considered to be in that area slightly below the navel. In order to make any stance stable yet flexible, strong yet springy, this center of control must be able to move without weakening its position. It is commonly accepted that the lower the center of balance the more stable an individual. This is not always true however; if the center of gravity is too low, one actually becomes too stable and cannot move easily since his mobility and flexibility are restricted.'

The late Bruce Lee was the foremost innovator of creative martial arts learning principles. By experimenting, he found that no one part of the body could be totally responsible for stability; each body segment must be taught to work together as part of a whole. Then the end result would be dynamic, physical force capable of moving constantly with speed, flexibility and stability without any loss of balance or control.

The conclusions arrived at concerning balance and stability are:

1. THE CENTER OF BALANCE IS IN THE LOWERED NAVEL POSITION. This lowered position is established by bending the knees thus dropping the navel area slightly. This axis and pivot point of motion between the upper and lower segments of the body can be developed by breathing down into the navel area using specific exercise (See Chapter 2).

2. THE UPPER TORSO SHOULD NEVER PRECEDE OR FOLLOW THE LOWER SEGMENTS OF THE BODY.

3. THE LEGS AND FEET MOVE THE BODY AS A SINGLE SEGMENT. (Single Unit Moving Principle, to be covered in this chapter.)

OPEN BI JONG
When Used; Outside the kill range
Body Position:

Stand loose and relaxed without any visible signs of readiness. Keep head erect and stand facing opponent. Centerline is fairly square to opponent with the upper torso leaning forward slightly so the energy will begin to flow forward. The hands (depending on your speed) will usually be somewhere in front of you (6—1,2) so that they can enter the perimeters quickly should the opponent attack. Both legs are bent slightly at the knees. A light springy feeling should be felt. The feet should be a comfortable distance apart. A comfortable distance can be determined by your ability to move in any direction from a relaxed position in a single motion without hesitation or the shifting of your balance. The lead foot should be your strong side (right-handed, right side: left-handed, left side). The reason you use your strong side is that this side is usually the most coordinated, strongest and often the fastest. Because the majority of people are right-handed, the right side will be referred to as the lead side. If you are left-handed, you will probably prefer your left side to lead. If this is the case, whenever the right side is mentioned, use your left side and reveise all the following directions.

The lead foot is slightly ahead of your rear foot with both feet pointing outward at a 45 degree angle. This 45 degree angle gives you more stability in all directions when absorbing an attack. If the feet are both pointed straight ahead,

6-1   6-2

your balance will be weak on the right and left side. The weight should be about 70% on the rear foot and 30% on the lead foot.

Mental Readiness:

Do not anticipate any particular action from your opponent. Just keep attentive to his body position, distance and emotional level so you can judge if an attack is eminent. A distinct feeling of calmness should be felt. Since you are not projecting your readiness to absorb an attack or commit one, your opponenfs defenses are not keyed. This keeps his weaknesses exposed. Also, by being relaxed and not anticipating motion, you allow your mind to distinguish between motion that is non-threatening and actions that call for a specific response.

Visual Focus

Do not fix your vision on any one part of your opponent. Try to establish a total view where you can see any motion whether it is from the upper torso or the feet. Your distance from your opponent will often determine your point of visual concentration. For example, if you know you cannot be reached by his hand, then your general attention will be focused towards his feet. If your opponent is in the outer perimeter, you will be concerned with the total opponent. If he is in the inner perimeter, you will center on his upper torso with your peripheral vision still being aware of the lower gate of the opponent.

Visual Focus Exercises'. To strengthen and sensitize peripheral vision.

1 • Exercise for Muscles

   A. Sit in a comfortable position. Face forward. Look as far as possible to the right, moving only your eyes. Then move your eyes as far as you can to the left. Alternate three times. Look straight ahead; close your eyes and rest.

   B. Repeat the above, this time moving your eyes up and down. Be sure to move only your eyes.

   C. Repeat, moving your eyes diagonally — up right and down left. Reverse. Close eyes and rest.

   D. Visualize a large clock directly in front of you. Your nose is fixed to the center of it. Fix your gaze first on 12 o'clock and then move slowly around the clock clockwise, stopping your eyes briefly at each number*

When your return to 12, gaze straight ahead, close your eyes and rest. Then repeat, this time moving around the clock counterclockwise. Close your eyes and rest. Do not strain your eyes, but move your eyes in the widest circle possible without moving your nose.

2. Exercise for Application

Stand in an Open Bi Jong. Your partner stands in front of you with his chest within the outer perimeter. He holds a striking pad in one hand close in front of his body (6—3). With the other hand, he makes simulated hand or leg strikes. He moves slowly at first and then picks up speed. Your vision should be dispersed in the area of your partner's chest. Do not visually lock onto any point. Keep your mind clear of anticipated movement. As soon as you see *or feel* an action from your partner, strike the pad. When you feel that it is easy to read and see his total motion, have your partner move in 15 degree segments to the side, with you maintaining the same forward position (6—4). As he moves to the side, you must keep your eyes forward with the vision dispersed. Your partner continues offensive action at each point. He keeps the striking pad in front of him. You must pivot your body and strike to the side as he changes positions. He will keep changing positions until you, because of restricted vision, can no longer react to his movement.

Open Bi Jong Exercise

Practice Area*.

Use a friend or dummy, or an object placed on the floor to represent your opponenfs position. If practicing with a dummy or other object, determine the kill range by using your leg length plus three inches as outlined in Chapter 4.

6-3   6-4

Exercise A:

Stand in a relaxed Open Bi Jong, slightly outside the kill range (6—5). In a single motion move quickly at least two feet to the left, turning slightly so you end up still facing your opponent (6—6). If in the Open Bi Jong your right foot is your lead foot, then you spring off of it landing on your left foot and quickly turning to face your opponent. Be sure to immediately move the right foot into a comfortable position so balance is main- tained (6—7).

Exercise B:

Practice as in Exercise A above, this time moving to the right. If in the Open Bi Jong your right foot is your lead foot, spring off your left foot.

Exercise C:

Practice as in Exercise A, this time moving straight back. You push off your lead foot with the rear foot staying close to the floor but moving back about two feet. It should feel like a low level jump.

Comments:

This exercise is to practice moving quickly from an Open Bi Jong position. By practice you will determine just how to stand in order to move in any direction.

CLOSED BI JONG

When Used

The Closed Bi Jong is a defensive stance used when attacking or being attacked. It is used inside the kill range — all gates are closed with a full attack to the opponent.

Comments:

For clarity in learning and for exercise purposes, this stance is being presented in a stationary position. In reality the

6-5

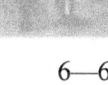
6—6

6-7

Closed Bi Jong is always in motion and conforms to your physique, speed, control and your opponenfs body position. (Application in Part 2).

Anytime either you or your opponent enter the kill range, all perimeters will close. This means that your centerline squares to the opponent. Your legs position themselves for creating a flexible but stable base and automatically assume a leg immobiliziiig position (6-8). This leg position is such that your lead leg angles toward and idways favors the opponenfs opposite leg. Your lead leg is always inside the opponent's leg to restrict his leg potential. This leg position plus the flowing of body energy th毗 is used in double direct closing (Part 2) is what causes the leg trapping principles. The hands enter their proper perimeter to control incoming energy. Simultaneous with all this is tiie projecting forward of your attacking energy.

Exercise Body Position:

Keep head erect and stand facing opponent. Legs are a comfortable distance apart; your strong foot is in the lead position and your rear leg is bent noticeably at the knee. The rear foot points outward about a 45 degree angle (6—9, 10). The rear foot may have a raised heel

6-8

6-9

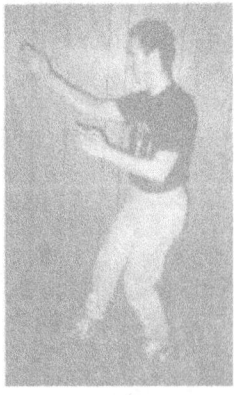

6-10

6-11

or stay flush to the ground depending on your body size. A light-framed individual may raise the rear heel (6—11). A large-framed person will normally keep both feet on the floor with his weight favoring the balls of his feet. His heels may actually spring lightly off the floor. In either case (by raising the rear heels or moving the weight to the balls of the feet), you load your energy forward thus making it easier to explode into your opponent.

    The lead leg is a comfortable distance in front of the body with the toes pointed in the same direction as the rear foot. The knee of the lead leg is bent and leans in towards the centerline. The weight should be distributed 80% on the rear leg and 20% on the front. This distribution will vary when applying technique. The turning of the lead leg in the same direction as the rear foot and the drawing the leg in towards the centerline cause a torquing action at the waist with the hips straining in the same direction as the feet. You can allow the hips to turn slightly in the direction of the feet, but the upper torso must keep the centerline. Lean forward slightly from the waist up; this will create a natural energy flow towards the opponent. The angle of lean is such that if you were in the proper Closed Bi Jong position and raised your lead leg, you would feel a slow falling-forward motion.
To keep your energy flow strong on one side, the lead hand should always be on the same side as the lead foot. The lead hand is extended forward at a slight inward angle, palm towards the centerline, with the forearm angling upward so the tips of the fingers of the open hand point at the oppo

nenfs eyes. The bend in the arm is such that the distance from the body to the elbow is the width of the extended fingers (6—12). The rear hand is lower and closer to the body. The elbow is out slightly and even with the front of the body. The forearm angles upward, palm towards the centerline, with the tips of the fingers in the open hand pointing towards the solar plexus of your opponent. Arms are relaxed with no tension or stiffness.

6-12

Applied Exercise:

Stand in an Open Bi Jong postion. Suddenly drop into a Closed Bi Jong. Immediately freeze the position and check it over for accuracy. Is the body angle right? Is the weight 80/20? Is the centerline proper? Are the hands extended properly? Are the feet pointed in the right direction and spaced a comfortable distance apart and are the knees bent? Is your mind clear of distractions and is your energy flowing towards the opponent?

Alternate Applied Exercise:

When walking relaxed, suddenly turn to the rear and drop into either a left or right Qosed Bi Jong. Exercises such as this help make a natural transition from a nondefensive position to a tight defensive-offensive position.

Comments:

You will not fight from this awkward position. It is only an exercise position that helps stretch tight muscles and develops certain lines of body motion. These lines complement leg immobilization techniques, trapping principles, and a natural forward flow of energy. Remember this is an exercise position, and will be a little awkward.

When practicing hand technique in Chapter 7, try to maintain the basic lines of the Closed Bi Jong but allow the body to relax and the weight distribution to be about 70% rear and 30% front. The centerline should always be maintained but the waist torque does not have to be as extreme as in the Closed Bi Jong exercise.

LEFT AND RIGHT AND REVERSE CLOSED BI JONG
When Used:

To absorb an attack from the side or rear.

Left Closed Bi Jong Exercise:

Stand upright with feet parallel and a little less than shoulder width apart. Keep the body relaxed and look straight ahead (6—13). In a single motion, push off of the right foot. At the same time, raise the left foot and step 12 inches to the left. As soon as you start your left motion, turn your head towards the opponent and begin to turn the body to the right so when

6-13

you step down on the left foot you are already turned halfway to the right (6—14). As your weight settles onto your left foot, your body should complete the turn with your right leg drawing up into a right Gosed Bi Jong position (6—15).

Simultaneous with your feet and body movement, the hands arc up so that they are in the Closed Bi Jong position when the body comes to rest. This technique is done in one smooth motion.

Right Closed Bi Jong Exercise:

To move to the right, switch the procedure for the left Closed Bi Jong. Push off of your left foot and end up in a left dosed Bi Jong position.

Reverse Gos^a Bi Jong Exercise:

Stand upright with feet parallel and slightly less than shoulder width apart. Using your left foot, step forward 24 inches. Just as the left foot touches the floor, spin your body around to the right arcing the hands up at the same time. You should make a full 180 degree turn to the right. As the balance draws up over the left foot, place the right in a Closed Bi Jong position. You should now be in a comfortable right Gosed Bi Jong. To end up in a left Closed Bi Jong, step forward with your right foot and pivot to the left.

Comments:

If you turn and face a possible side attack without moving away, you expose yourself to immediate danger (6—16). By moving away and arcing your arms up as you turn, you clear the area of potential incoming energy plus you force your opponent to take an extra step because of the added distance.

6-14

6-15

6-16

Left Closed Bi Jong Applied Exercise:

Stand in an Open Bi Jong position. Your opponent stands directly to your right side on the edge of the kill range (6—17). Keep your eyes straight ahead. Whenever your partner is ready he suddenly reaches forward and tries to touch you on the shoulder. (This will simulate an attack.) As soon as you see or sense his attack, you move to the opposite side (6—18), slip into a right Closed Bi Jong and end up facing your opponent (6—19). Arc your hands up as you turn. If you do not react well when the opponent attacks, have him move 5 degrees around towards the front and do it again.

It is not important to see your opponent clearly to respond. Learn to withdraw to vague but quick motion that could be threatening to you. Remember these are exercises to help you develop natural but effective defensive reactions that can be quickly turned into an offensive technique.

Right Closed Bi Jong Applied Exercise:

Repeat as above except your opponent stands to your left side and you move to your right ending up in a left Closed Bi Jong.

Reverse Closed Bi Jong Applied Exercise:

Repeat as above except your opponent stands behind you. You have the option of stepping forward with either your right or left foot and ending up in either a left Closed Bi Jong or a right Closed Bi Jong.

6-17

6—18

6-19

SINGLE UNIT MOVING TECHNIQUE
Purpose:

To maintain constant control of balance and the direction of energy flow, and to preserve a stable base for exploding striking power. This technique will be practiced in two ways: Exercise 1:

Assume a right Closed Bi Jong position (6—20). Without leaning any more forward, raise your right foot slightly off the floor and begin to step forward about six inches (6—21). The left foot pushes the body forward and as the right foot settles back to the floor, the left foot snaps forward six inches so a Closed Bi Jong position is once more established (6—22). The total action should be quick and smooth. It is not a jump. It is more like flowing across the floor. The legs simply move the body forward, rather than the upper torso moving forward on its own. Keep the hands up and the centerline constant.

To develop more flexibility in your moves, switch back and forth from a right Closed Bi Jong to a left Closed Bi Jong by simply allowing the left side to come forward while withdrawing the right side to the rear position. Learning to alternate from a right to left Closed Bi Jong will give you more versatility when following any evasive action of your opponent.

6-20　　　　　　　6-21　　　　　　　6-22

Exercise 2 (Duck Walk):

Bend the left knee while raising your right foot off the floor (6—23). Keep the upper torso straight. Step forward about 12 inches onto the right foot while quickly lifting the left foot off the floor (6—24), Then repeat by stepping onto the left foot, then the right, and so on. In order to have the opportunity to practice balance control, keep the raised foot off the floor for about 5 seconds. Do not lean forward or backward at any time. The only action is done by the stepping motion of the legs. The motion can be to the right or left and the rear following the same stepping type of action. Your hands can remain by your sides or assume a comfortable forward position.

Comments:

This exercise teaches the body not to extend forward. It trains the legs to move the body into position so a constant power load can be maintained (See Part 2, Power Base). This power load is not only a key principle to Phon Sao (Trapping Hands) and Chi Sao (Sticking Hands), but also is critical in the constant flow of energy during applied technique.

6-23

6-24

QUESTIONS — STANCES
1. List 3 points that are critical for maintaining proper balance and weight distribution.
2. What are the body positions in the Open Bi Jong?
3. What angle are the feet pointed in the Open Bi Jong?
4. Name 2 reasons why you lead with your strong side.
5. What is the reason for an Open Bi Jong?
6. Where are your thoughts in Open Bi Jong?
7. Where is your vision directed in Open Bi Jong?
8. If you have a friend to practice with, how can you practice the Open Bi Jong exercise?
9. When do you use the Closed Bi Jong position?
10. What happens to your energy in the Closed Bi Jong when you lean slightly forward?
11. Name 2 things you can do to reduce danger of an attack from the side.
12. Which foot do you push off of when you move quickly to the right?
13. Describe the physical principle of the single unit moving technique.

CHAPTER 7
BASIC HAND PRINCIPLES

The hands open the door to all of your potential.

PERIMETER CONTROL: BLOCKING VS. CLEARING THE GATE
To effectively control your perimeter, the hands and feet must learn to react in the most efficient manner

Blocking
Blocking is a reaction used to intercept your opponent\ specific technique with a direct opposing technique without precise control over your perimeter. The block can be overextended towards the action of the opponent (chasing the strike, 7—0) which may be exactly what the opponent wants. Blocking is usually done as a stiff expression of energy to counter incoming offensive energy.

Example of Blocking
Your opponent uses a right hook towards your head. Your hand goes up to block the hook, leaving your rib area exposed. Your opponent drops in with a low strike to the ribs which you are unable to intercept in time to avoid being hit (7—1).

Limitation of Blocking
If the opponent draws you out of your perimeter or off balance, it is difficult to strike fast or effectively until you regain your perimeters and a stable base.

Clearing the Gate
Clearing the gate means that any offensive action, by the opponent, that tries to enter your inner perimeter causes your hand to intercept, redirect, deflect or absorb the in-

7-0

7-1

coming energy. Feinting or distracting actions by the opponent are incomplete motions outside the primary or inner perimeter and pose no actual threat.

Example of Clearing the Gate

Your opponent uses a right hook towards your head. Your hand goes up in a high Taun Sao to the edge of your upper perimeter. Your opponent drops in with a low strike to your ribs which you intercept with a Goang Sao or a Die Jeong. Since the motion of your high Taun Sao is confined to the edge of the upper perimeter, your elbow is low enough to restrict low strikes (7—2). In clearing the gate, balance is always maintained because of the controlled motion; therefore it is easy to do offensive and defensive technique at the same time.

GENERAL COMMENTS - HAND TECHNIQUES

Unless otherwise stated, the starting practice distance between you and your partner for applied hand exercise will be a full arm's length. You will be facing each other. As stated in Chapter 6, you can maintain a loose Closed Bi Jong position for any hand exercises that call for a Closed Bi Jong.

In application, each defensive technique is paired with an offensive action. In this chapter, for the purpose of training each hand to act independently of the other only the defensive response will be explained. The offensive action will be dealt with in Part 2.

SUPERIOR AND INFERIOR POSITIONS

Superior Position

In the superior position, your hands are over the opponent's wrist-forearm area (7—3). In this position, it is easy to redirect the opponent's energy with a minimum of effort. It is ideal for setting up trapping-striking technique. Also, it is a tight defensive position since the opponent must exert an extra

7-2

Inferior Position
In an inferior position, your energy is underneath the opponent^ energy (7-3). The angles of the attack are limited; since the opponent has the leverage of pressure and the advantage of direct line attack, your energy flow towards the opponent is restricted. You must go around his energy or force through it. The inferior position is a very difficult position to defend from since you must use twice the strength and twice the movement.

PALM PHON SAO
Purpose
By touching the opponent and applying slight pressure, you are able to read his movements and restrict the angles of his motion.
Phon Sao Hand Exercise Positions
Only the superior position will be practiced, since at this basic level, the inferior position is only an exercise position. **Exercise 1**
Initially, practice palm Phon Sao with only one arm.
Use a cupped palm (7—4). This creates a natural trap and makes it difficult for the opponent to move. Your fingers arc around the opponenfs wrist with the heel of your hand on the underside of his wrist. Your fingers have a *slight* squeezing pressure around the wrist. Your elbow pulls in slightly towards your centerline. Your forearm extends out with a slight angle upward. The

7-3　　　　　　7-4

arm is firm but not stiff (7-5). Once you have the feeling of the position, practice using both arms.

Comments

This is a primary hand position for natural trapping principles. When you apply the lines of directive energy flow, the opponent will find it difficult to do direct offensive techniques from this position. Directive energy flow will be covered in Volume 2.

Exercise 2

Picture 7—6 shows a variation of the superior palm Phon Sao hand position. This position is used for exercises. In this position your hands do not cup around the opponenfs wrists. They lie on the top section of the opponent's wrists so a minimum of restriction is placed on the opponenfs movement. This extra freedom for your opponent allows him to move much easier; you therefore must be much quicker in your reactions. Your hands should press downwards slightly so that you are able to read the opponenfs movement.

TAUN SAO

Purpose

Taun Sao is used to clear and protect the upper perimeter. It is used only in the upper perimeter (by the right hand in the right perimeter and the left hand in the left perimeter). Exercise Position

Keep your body square. Using your primary arm, place

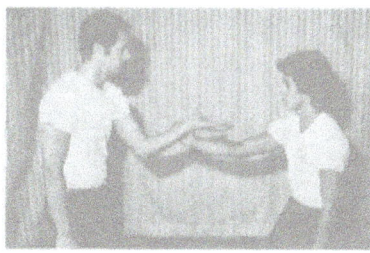
7-5

7-6

your elbow on or as close to the centerline as possible. Keep your forearm parallel to the floor and pointing straight ahead with palm open and facing up. Your elbow is slightly out from your body (7—7 and 8). There should be a distinct strain felt in your shoulder. If no strain is felt, move your elbow farther away from your body, keeping your forearm parallel to the floor and on the centerline.

Comments

This exercise position loosens the shoulder muscles. Flexible shoulder muscles allow you a higher degree of motion in the upper perimeter; tight and restrictive muscles could cause you to violate the centerline principle, since you have to adjust your body to compensate for the tight muscles. Taun Sao can be used anywhere within its own upper permimeter. **Taun Sao Application Principles**

A primary Aikido principle states that you point where you want your energy to go. This principle has a way of extending your energy out of the arm and towards the target. In order to get the maximum from this primary principle, a Wing Chun Do hand torquing technique is added as seen in the applications below.

Outer Taun Sao

Purpose:

Outer Taun Sao is used to clear the upper perimeter from the inside to the outer edge.

Exercise:

Stand in an Open Bi Jong. Your right arm comes up

7-7   7-8

in a loose but swift action, palm facing down. Your elbow raises slightly towards the opponent with the forearm making a clockwise sweeping motion. This motion is directed toward the centerline of the upper perimeter. There is little elbow motion other than its forward action (7—9). By moving forward, the elbow extends the forearm out so that the opponent's incoming energy is intercepted at a safe distance. By limiting side movement, the elbow acts as a hinge from which the forearm can arc its energy up or down without endangering the upper perimeter. This forward elbow position is referred to as the primary elbow position since it allows the maximum use of the forearm-hand techniques.

The forearm, remaining loose, arcs to the right edge of the upper perimeter as fast as possible to clear the perimeter. The hand is open and facing the centerline (7—10). A split second before intercepting the invading energy, the hand suddenly flips over. The palm faces upward and a burst of concentrated energy shoots out the tips of your fingers. At the same time, the whole arm springs forward a little ending up in a slight angle upward (7-11). A sudden and short burst of tension appears upon contact with the opponent's arm. This tension is caused by the quick tightening and jerking forward of your arm muscles. This burst of tightness lasts only a fraction of a second. It acts to explode your energy out your hand and deflect the opponenfs

7-9

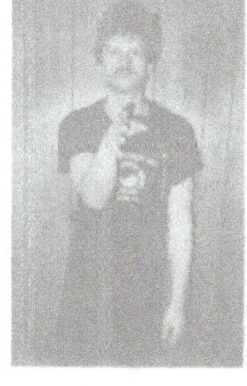
7-10

7-11

energy. From this dynamic action springs the next technique, either striking or trapping.

Inner Taun Sab

Purpose

Inner Taun Sao is used to clear the upper perimeter from outer edge to centerline.

Exercise

Stand with your arms by your sides. Your primary arm raises loose and relaxed. Your hand is open and loose with palm facing down (7-12). Your elbow raises upward. The line to follow when raising the arm is the *outer edge* of the opponenfs upper perimeter. This allows you to be just far enough out to scoop his energy in a snapping action towards the centerline without exposing your own perimeter too much.

When your hand reaches the shoulder height of the opponent (7—13) quickly snap your hand over in a short hacking motion at the opponent's arm. At the same time, move the whole arm inward and slightly forward so that in the finished position you are pointing your fingers at the opponent's eyes (7-14).

Comments

Both outer and inner Taun Sao are paired with an appropriate striking technique (Part 2) · The selection of which Taun Sao to use is instinctive. Only practice will lay the base for a proper reaction to fit a particular situation. Common sense tells you not to use an inner Taun Sao against a wide arc hook, because you would have to reach too far to contact it. A lot depends on the position of your hands when the incoming energy starts. If they are outside, toward the centedine, you would most likely use an outer Taun Sao. If your hands are by your side, you could use either one.

7-12   7-13   7—14

Taun Sao Exercises

Before beginning these exercises, refer to the General Comments —Hand Techniques at the beginning of this chapter. *Exercise* 4

Stand in an Open Bi Jong in front of your opponent. Put your arms by your side and just relax. Disperse your focus over the opponent (7-15). The opponent has two options: he can simulate a strike to your head by either a hooking (7—16) or a straight punch (7—17).

To begin the exercise, he will identify which arm and which strike he will use. This will give you an opportunity to concentrate on the basic lines of the Taun Sao, so you can make corrections each time if needed. The opponent will move slowly at first to allow you to practice developing arm-body coordination. As you smooth out your reaction, allow the opponent to speed up each strike. Next, allow him to strike with either a hooking or a straight punch without any warning of which punch -he will use. Then allow him to punch with either hand using either strike, without telling you in advance.

Use only an arm action since this technique is only one part of a series of explosive motions. Develop a natural motion that has no jerking or unnecessary body action. Teach your arms the basic move and do not anticipate your opponent's motion; then the arms will respond on their own to your opponent's move without thinking of what to do.

Do not exceed your perimeter. Once you develop a smooth Taun Sao, practice perimeter control by having your opponent fake a hook or a straight punch. See if you can control your motion by stopping within the perimeter.

7-15

7-16

7-17

Exercise 5

This exercise combines palm Phon Sao Exercise 2 position with Taun Sao. Exercise palm Phon Sao is used only to read the opponent's hooking motion. This gives you the opportunity to practice reacting with a strong Taun Sao.

Place your hands in a superior position but do not cup around opponent's wrist. (Use the Exercise 2 palm Phon Sao, 7—6). Your opponent begins the exercise from the inferior position. He has the option of moving with the right hand (7—18), the left hand, or both hands (7—19). He hooks around and touches the side of your head. You respond only to his striking hand. When in an extended palm Phon Sao position, your hands must maintain a slight pressure downward. Your opponent must apply a little upward pressure in the starting position. He must always return to his original inferior position before starting his next move. He can move fast or slow or vary his speed to increase your concentration. In order to insure that you apply light pressure to his forearms at all times, the opponent also has the option of striking at your midsection from his inferior position. If you are applying downward pressure, it will automatically deflect his blow.

Do not go outside your upper perimeter when Taun Saoing. Snap your Taun Sao hand over at contact in order to practice the proper angles of motion and the

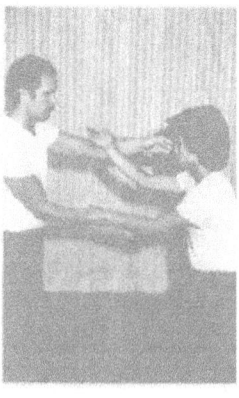 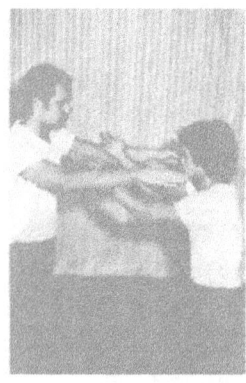

7-18   7-19

proper use of concentrated energy flow. Your opponent must make his hooks in a short arc over your arms; this will make you respond quickly.

This exercise helps you develop snapping Taun Saos that react automatically to incoming motion. It also starts developing your use of touch responses. This is not a competitive exercise; it must be done at a speed which will allow you to recognize mistakes so you can eliminate them.

Exercise C

This is an advanced Taun Sao-Phon Sao exercise. It is to be done blindfolded. Comfortably cover your eyes so that your vision is completely blocked. Follow the basic Taun Sao-Phon Sao Exercise B given above (7—20A). Your opponent can also strike at your midsection (7—20B). Practice this exercise two minutes. Then switch and let your partner be superior and practice his Taun Sao.

FOOK SAO

Purpose

Fook Sao is an arm trapping and drawing technique. It is primarily used when an interception or block leaves your energy in a high superior position.

Exercise Position

1. Place your left arm in a Taun Sao exercise position (7—21). Keep your fingers together. Raise your fingers up; then strain them down towards your forearm (7—22). Rotate your hand over 180 degrees clockwise. At all times keep the strain in your wrist. When rotating the hand, your wrist should raise a little so there is a slight angle upward to the forearm (7—23). This exercise loosens, strengthens and de-

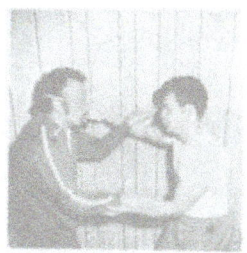
7-20A

7-20B

7-21

velops more flexibility in the wrist.

2. To further develop the wrist, do Exercise 1, this time continuing the rotation of the hand in a clockwise position. As the hand moves to the extreme left, open the fingers and strain them outwards (7—24). Continue the arc until the hand returns to a finished position, hand vertical to the floor and fingers together (7—25). Maintain the strain at all times. While the hand is rotating, the wrist will stay on the centerline. This complete exercise will be referred to as the Taun Sao-Fook Sao-Pak Sao exercise (TS-FS-PS Exercise).

Fook Sao Applied Exercise

Stand in a right, relaxed Closed Bi Jong with your opponent in ready position. Extend your left ann in a simulated vertical fist position. Your opponent blocks with an outer Taun Sao movement (7-26). As soon as your opponent's arm contacts yours, quickly circle your open p+m around his arm, applying pressure against his inner forearm. This creates a pocket between your fingers and

7-22

7-23

7-24

7-25

7-26

7-27

7-28

your forearm (7—27). At the same time you are applying pressure, draw your arm downward about 12 inches and slightly towards you (7—28). Use a quick jerking motion. Be sure to maintain a constant pressure on his arm. The Fook Sao is an arm action that can be strengthened by drawing your upper torso down a little to add to the Fook Sao jerk. Keep your centerline constant.

GOANGSAO

Purpose

This is a low arm sweeping technique used to clear your lower perimeter and lower gate.

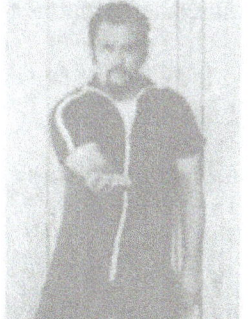

7-29

Exercise Position

Place your right hand in the Taun Sao[1] exercise position (7—29). The hand arcs downward on the centerline (7—30) and then sweeps outward in a firm action coming to rest at the outer edge of the right perimeter (7—31). There is a slight bend in the elbow and wrist. The bend in the wrist creates the wrist pocket. The finished arm position is approximately 45 degrees away from the body (7—32). As a rule, the Goang Sao, when completed, will immediately return to a Closed Bi Jong or Taun Sao position. This allows you to practice bringing the

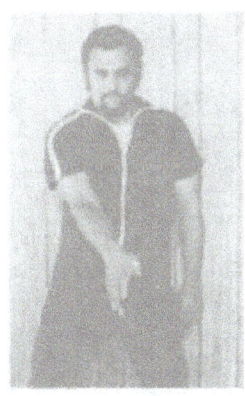

7-30

7-31

7-32

energy back into the upper perimeter.

Goang Sao Application

Goang Sao may be used against a front thrust kick or a low hand strike. The incoming energy is trapped in the wrist pocket. Goang Sao, when applied, will always be paired with offensive techniques.

Starting Position

Assume a right relaxed Closed Bi Jong. Your opponent is an arm's length away (7—33).

Exercise

Your opponent drops down slightly and jabs into your ribs with his left hand (7—34). Without moving your body forward, lean your upper torso slightly fb☐ ward as your right arm arcs downward into Goang Sao (7—35). Stay within your perimeter. The Goang Sao, after sweeping contact, immediately returns to your upper perimeter. Practice this until you have developed smooth action. Then allow your opponent to fake a strike so you can develop perimeter control.

Comments

The bends at the wrist and elbow allow for absorption of

7-33

7-34

7—35

shock to the arm. They also give more flexibility for followup techniques. This technique should be done with a quick snapping action. Since the upper perimeter becomes exposed for a moment, this return must be immediate.

DIE JEONG
Puipose

This is a downward palm blocking action. It is used primarily in the lower perimeter and gate. It also may be used in the upper perimeter when your hands are high and inside the opponent*s upper perimeter.

Exercise Position

Assume a relaxed Closed Bi Jong exercise position (7—36). In a single action, drop your right arm straight down, torquing the palm firmly downward as you contact the imaginary opponent (7—37). Do not lock your elbow; your arm should not be straight. If the opponent kicks into your hand, this could cause injury to the wrist and elbow joint. Always allow a slight bend in your elbow to absorb shock.

If the technique is to be used against a low kick or block, then as the arm drops, bend the knees. This causes the body to lower thus allowing both for a lower Die Jeong and the use of firm body energy in the block.

Die Jeong Applied

Strike high to your opponent's head (7—38). While you are striking, your opponent suddenly drops and strikes for your ribs. You must react when his body drops or it will be too

7-36

7-37

late. In a single action, your body flows with him as he drops, and your palm Die Jeongs downward and slightly forward (7-39).

Comments

A Die Jeong is always done with a quick, snapping action. The hand, after completing the Die Jeong, immediately bounces back into the upper perimeter in the fsm of another technique. Do not break your centerline or lean over when doing Die Jeong. Simply drop the body in a springy motion by bending the knees and immediately recovering.

As in the Goang Sao, your opponent may fake a strike so you can practice controlling your downward motion.

7-38

7-39

PAK SAO

Purpose

Pak Sao clears the upper perimeter. It is used primarily to deflect the opponenfs energy across his body. When the term "Pak Sao" is used it refers to either the act of clearing the upper perimeter or the position of the hand in front of the upper body. This hand acts defensively while the other hand is involved in a technique.

Pak Sao Exercise

Place your hands by your sides (7—40). Raise your right arm forward and upward just on the outer edge of the opponenfs upper perimeter (7—41). Keep your arm relaxed and your hand loose. Just as your hand reaches shoulder height of

7—40

the opponent, snap the hand so that it is perpendicular to the floor. Firm up the palm and spring it to the centerline with a smashing action (7—42). Your hand stops on the centerline. In the finish position, your hand is out about 12 inches from your body with the palm perpendicular to the floor.

Comments

The Pak Sao will stay only on the side it is initiated. After you have contacted your opponent's energy, there is no reason to cross over the centerline. Once your hand reaches the centerline, the opponent's energy cannot strike you. Moving farther across the centerline would open a potential elbow attack. You do not need strength in this technique; speed of motion by itself will be sufficient.

Pak Sao Applied Exercise

Your opponent is in a ready position. You start in an Open Bi Jong, your hands by your sides. Stand an arm's length away from the opponent (7—43). At first, tell the opponent which arm to use so you can practice your lines of motion. The opponent moves slowly at first; he will only speed up when you feel you are ready. With-

7-41

7-42

7y3

out telegraphing his movement, the opponent tries to touch you on the upper chest with his left hand. As soon as you see or feel your opponent move, your arm moves up in a snapping, arcing action to sweep the upper right perimeter clear. Your palm (perpendicular to the floor) will not go past the centerline.

Your right hand reacts to his left and your left to his right. If you misjudge occasionally and intercept right to right or left to left, it is all right, if you recover rapidly and do not do it too often.

The speed of the Pak Sao and the angle of motion when you contact your opponent should bounce his arm to the opposite side of his body.

Refine your motion to a natural reaction on both right and left sides. Then, without indicating which one, the opponent may strike with either hand. He may add more speed as you develop better reactions. If he can touch you each time before you can react, he should step back a couple of inches and strike from there. If, at his top speed, you can intercept his motion without difficulty, he should move forward slightly. This will shorten the distance and cause you to move faster to intercept his strike.

Do not allow your opponent to strike with both hands at the same time. There should always be a pause between his strikes so that you have time to assume a ready position. Once you feel confident in your Pak Sao, have the opponent fake a punch; see if you clear the upper gate or chase the opponenfs energy. When the opponent fakes, you simply should draw your hand up into the upper perimeter and maintain a closed gate. If he changes the angle of his attack, you should be able to follow his next move with a minimum of motion. Also, since your defensive actions are always paired with an offensive motion, you will have hit him by the time he starts his second move.

LOP SAO
Purpose

Lop Sao is used to physically draw the opponent off balance.

Lop Sao Exercise

1. *Outside Technique*

Assume a relaxed Closed Bi Jong position. Your opponent extends his right arm. You extend your right arm so that the outside of your wrist touches the outside of your partner's right wrist (7—44). In a single action, turn your hand down (7-45), grasp the opponenfs wrist (7-46) at the wrist joint, and draw his arm outward 45 degrees (7—47) and down at

7-44

7-45

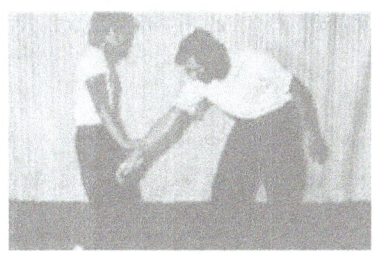

7—46

7-47

7-48

118

a 45 degree angle (7—48). Pivot your centerline to account for his changed position.

Grasp his wrist as shown in 7—46. Apply a firm, squeezing pressure between your thumb and forefingers. This pressure will be sufficient to maintain a strong hold, but if the opponent should jerk his arm back, your hand should slip off. This will allow you to continue with other technique. If you grab his wrist too firmly and he jerks his arm back, you will be pulled toward him and loose control momentarily.

When you turn your hand to grasp his wrist, you may find yourself a little high of the wrist joint. Allow your grasp to slip down to the wrist joint as you begin the drawing action. Do not Lop Sao while holding onto his upper arm. This calls for a tight grip since the forearm is hard to grasp because of its thickness.

Once you have the basic movement refined, practice speeding up your grasping and drawing action. Allow your opponent to jerk his wrist away when he feels you move. ITiis will make you move in a shorter motion so as not to telegraph your action.

2. *Inside Technique*

The opponent stands in a relaxed Closed Bi Jong. You assume a relaxed Closed Bi Jong. Extend your right hand in a simulated strike to the opponenfs face. The opponent raises his left hand and touches the outside of your forearm as if to block (7—49). Turn your right hand down, grasp his wrist (open fingers) and pull down with a snapping action while striking with the left hand (7—50). The turning of the palm and the grasping are the same as the outside Lop Sao. The drawing action is at a 45 degree angle down but only about 30 degrees

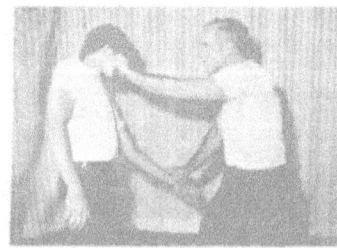

7-49

7-50

out. If the opponent should block your left hand as you are striking (7—51), you can do an inner Lop Sao with the left hand and strike with your right (7—52).

Comments

Lop Sao neutralizes the opponent's hand and exposes him for a split second to your strike.

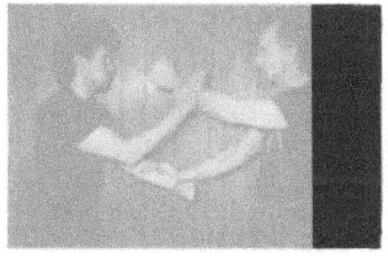 

7-51   7-52

BONG SAO
Purpose

Bong Sao redirects the opponenfs energy. It is used primarily when you are already in contact with the opponenfs energy. At first it is an unnatural and awkward move, but it will become natural and smooth with practice. It is extremely useful for close range defensive motion. It also sets up your opponent for the next technique.

7-53   7-54

Exercise Position

Start in a Taun Sao exercise position (7—53). In a single action, rotate the elbow counterclockwise in a short arc (7—54) to the height of your shoulder. Your elbow points straight ahead of your shoulder. The forearm and hand twist over and raise only until they are a 45 degree angle downward. The hand (back of the hand on the centerline) continues to torque over (7—55) creating a feeling that your body is lifting up slightly; this feeling complements the redirecting of your opponent's energy. The forearm moves in the same motion forward to a 45 degree angle from the body (7—56). The elbow locks holding this position while the arm pivots at the shoulder under the incoming energy.

To practice the shoulder hinge, move the finished Bong Sao across the body as far as it will go. This helps the shoulder become more flexible. Keep the centerline constant at all times.

Comments

Bong Sao is usually coupled with inner Pak Sao so a trapping technique can be applied.

Be sure you understand the two 45 degree positions of the forearm, the palm twisting and the shoulder hinge. These points are necessary to create a natural redirecting of the opponent's energy. When doing Bong Sao, *do not allow your forearm to drop back towards your body.* The closer your forearm comes to your body the more difficult it becomes to counter the opponenfs forward energy.

7-55   7-56

Bong Sao Applied

Your hand starts in the inferior position, the opponenfs energy over yours (7—57). Suddenly the opponent strikes upward towards your head with his left hand. As you feel the energy lifting, you follow, arcing into a Bong Sao (7-58). Bong Sao will only move inward until your hand touches the centerline (7—59). This should be sufficient to have redirected the opponent's energy to a nonoffensive angle (7—60, note arrow). Yet your own gate should not be open for either an elbow technique or a lower strike. Your other hand, at the same time you Bong Sao, will go up into an inner Pak Sao position in between the opponent's hand and your body (7—61). This will set him up for trapping combinations.

7-57

7-58

7-59

7-60

7-61

HUENG SAO
Purpose

Hueng Sao* is a body trapping technique using a circular open-handed motion.

Hueng Sao Exercise Position

Stand in an Open Bi Jong position. Fully extend your right arm. Place your hand in a closed fist position at the height and center of your nose (7—62). In a single action, open the palm and arc the right arm across the centerline as if circling around your opponenfs shoulder. Move only to the left edge of your body (7—63). Then curve the arc in quickly and stop so the wrist is on the centerline. The hand turns and faces the right side (7—64). The arm will lock at the shoulder and elbow. The elbow and wrist will be slightly bent. The left hand raises in a striking action.

Hueng Sao Applied

Imagine you have just finished striking the opponent's

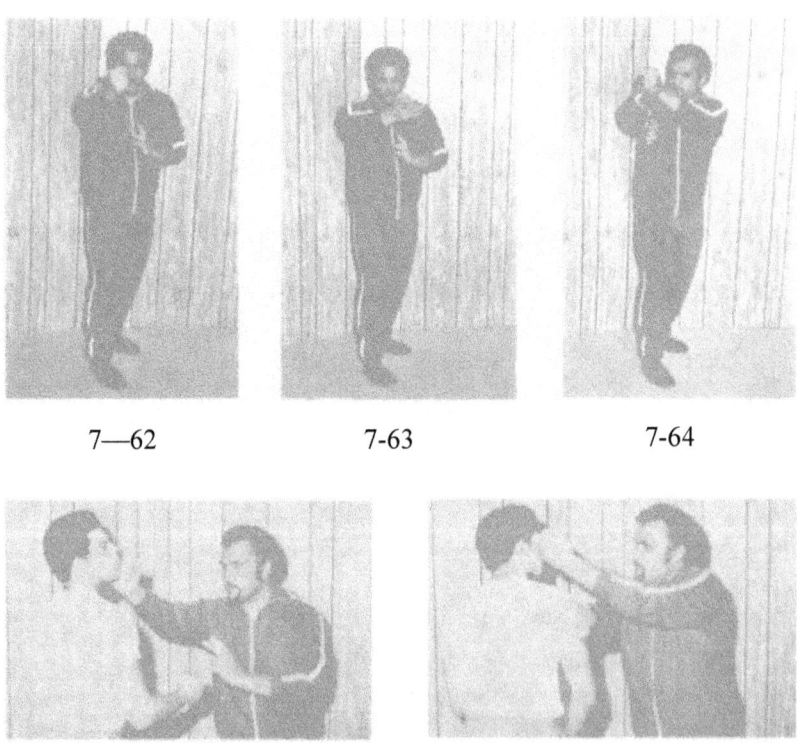

7—62   7-63   7-64

7-65   7-66

face with the right hand (7—65) and you wish to strike him again while minimizing his technique to block you. The right hand will quickly arc around his right biceps and create a steady pressure to your right while your left hand strikes without interference. There will be a slight shift of the opponent to the right as you apply pressure so adjust your body position to keep your centerline straight (7—66).
Comments

This technique must be done very quickly so the opponent cannot shift and correct his balance. Keeping your center- line constant will give you control of the opponenfs body energy. This will allow you to easily use follow-up techniques.

7-67

BIL JEE
Purpose

Bil Jee is a finger thrust to the eyes. It is used to draw out the opponent's energy so that you can trap it. It can also be used to block incoming energy.

Bil Jee Exercise Position

Stand in an Open Bi Jong position. Keep both arms relaxed by your sides (7—67). Raise the right hand, palm facing left side. Move your hand across the body to just slightly past your centerline (7-68). As the hand moves across, it arcs upward and forward with the

7-68

7-69

7-70

palm open, relaxed and facing the left side. The hand arcs up towards the opponent's face until the hand reaches about throat height (7—69). The hand then snaps over (palm down); the arm suddenly straightens out; and the fingers project towards the opponent's eyes (7—70). When the arm straightens, the upper torso leans slightly forward. This body movement helps extend the fingers forward. The fingers only jab at the eyes and then recoil immediately 4 to 6 inches. As the right hand begins its move, the left hand raises up in a loose Bi Jong position.

Double Bil Jee Exercise and Application

Double Bil Jee is a reaction to the opponenfs block of a single Bil Jee.

Practice the right Bil Jee as in the exercise above. As the right Bil Jee is blocked (7—71), the left hand suddenly springs forward underneath, slightly touching the right forearm. It moves up so that for a split second, a pocket is created, trapping the opponent's energy (7-72). From this pocket any number of striking techniques can be employed — left finger thrust, left Lop Sao with right Qua Choie, left single vertical fist (7-73).

Comments

Any time you strike at the opponent's eyes, it causes the opponent to naturally react to protect them. This reaction commits him for a moment while you close the gap and set him up for another technique. When doing double Bil Jee, do not allow

7-71

7-72

7-73

the pocket to exist for more than a split second since the opponent can push downward and trap both your hands.

Bil Jee and double Bil Jee are primarily used to draw out and trap the opponent. Unless you train your fingers for it, it is too easy to injure an extended finger when doing a snapping technique.

QUESTIONS — BASIC HAND PRINCIPLES

1. How can you effectively control your perimeters?
2. What is the difference between blocking and clearing the gate?
3. Name two disadvantages to the inferior hand position.
4. What advantage does touching your opponent with a slight pressure give you?
5. Why is a cupped hand position important when your hands are on the opponent's wrists?
6. What is Taun Sao's primary use?
7. What is the difference between inner and outer Taun Sao?
8. Give two reasons for using Fook Sao.
9. In what perimeter(s) is Goang Sao used?
10. What do you call a downward palm strike or block?
11. What two purposes does Pak Sao serve?
12. To what angles do you draw your opponent when using an inside Lop Sao?
13. Describe Bong Sao and its purpose.
14. What is Hueng Sao?
15. Explain applied double Bil Jee.
16. What is the primary purpose of single Bil Jee?

TRAINING SCHEDULE

technique	mon	tue	wed	thu	fri	sat	sun

www.ingramcontent.com/pod-product-compliance
Lightning Source LLC
Chambersburg PA
CBHW070946230426

43666CB00011B/2575